FIVE POLYPHONIC MASSES

BY HEINRICH ISAAC

Five Polyphonic Masses
By Heinrich Isaac

Transcribed and Edited from the Formschneider
First Edition (Nürnberg, 1555)
by

Louise Cuyler

ANN ARBOR
THE UNIVERSITY OF MICHIGAN PRESS

Library of Congress Catalog Card No. 56-7145

Paperback ISBN : 978-0-472-75090-0

Printed in the United States of America by Sequoia Press

This volume is respectfully dedicated

to

DR. KURT SACHS

revered scholar and treasured friend

PREFACE

SCHOLARLY RESEARCH in music of the fifteenth and sixteenth centuries has brought forth cumulative evidence of a rich creative activity among composers residing in England and on the continent in those centuries. Especially is this true of the works of Heinrich Isaac, a composer of Low Country birth, who worked in Italy and Austria, and whose stature as a creative artist can now be evaluated by the listener through live performances and recordings, as well as by the historian who examines the printed page of his music.

Much of Isaac's sacred music was published in Volumes V and XVI of *Denkmäler der Tonkunst in Oesterreich*, around the turn of the century. More recent publications, both in 1950, are transcriptions of his *CHORALIS CONSTANTINUS BOOK III*, by Dr. Louise E. Cuyler (University of Michigan Press) and *MISSA CARMINUM* in *DAS CHORWERK* series, under the general editorship of Friedrich Blume. These *FIVE POLYPHONIC MASSES*, also transcribed and edited by Dr. Louise E. Cuyler, and published by the University of Michigan Press, attest to the continued interest in bringing his music to life by preparing modern performance editions of the sacred compositions of this great master.

Special significance attaches to these later publications, since they are transcribed for use of present-day choral organizations. The *FIVE MASSES* which comprise this second volume by Dr. Cuyler are equally effective for concert performances or liturgical use, since they conform in every particular to the ideals expressed in the *Motu Proprio* of 1903 and the more recent pronouncement by Pope Pius XII.

Music is a living art. Its beauty must be realized through performance. Choral compositions of composers of the later centuries have long been available in editions suitable for performance and on records. Evidence of lively interest in the high quality of the music of Isaac already published is observed in the fact that choral groups have already made recordings of excerpts from the two 1950 editions of transcriptions referred to above.

It is a pleasure to express appreciation to the Horace H. Rackham School of Graduate Studies for making possible the publication of *FIVE MASSES* as a further contribution of the University of Michigan to musicological research, and toward fuller knowledge and keener appreciation of Heinrich Isaac as a composer.

EARL V. MOORE

Gratitude is expressed to the British Museum, from whom the microfilm of the *Choralis Constantinus* was procured.

L. C.

CONTENTS

Five Polyphonic Masses
by Heinrich Isaac

HISTORICAL AND ANALYTICAL COMMENTARY

THE MASS was framework and inspiration for much of the finest European music from earliest Christian times through the sixteenth century. Even in later years, only the symphony has ever rivaled the Mass in usefulness, adaptability, and persistence. From the earliest plain-song guise in Milanese and Roman liturgies especially, through the detached Mass movements in expanding polyphony of St. Martial and Notre Dame, to glorious fulfillment in the works of the Flemings, Italians, and Spaniards in the sixteenth century, the Mass is palpable record of a thousand-year evolution in musical style. Even in the three and a half centuries since the close of the great polyphonic era, few great composers have failed to utilize the Mass form at least once.

The liturgy of the Mass accrued gradually, but has undergone almost no significant changes since the fourteenth century. The text comprises two major divisions: the constant, unchangeable portion, called the Ordinary, and the occasional-seasonable portion, called the Proper. Each of these major sections has separated traditionally into those texts that may be sung[1] and those that are simply recited or spoken. Obviously, only the first of these categories has been of interest to composers.

The principal choral components of the Mass, in the order of their occurrence, are:

Ordinary	*Proper*
	1. Introit
2. Kyrie	
3. Gloria	
	4. Gradual[2]
	5. Alleluia or Tract
	6. Sequence[3]
7. Credo	
	8. Offertory
9. Sanctus (with Benedictus)	
10. Agnus Dei	
	11. Communion

All these texts have been the basis of compositions by musicians of every generation. Before the fourteenth century, parts of the Proper, being generally of more ancient origin, were most often chosen. Since the middle of the fourteenth century, however, composers have preferred the five texts of the Ordinary, doubtless because they are suitable for use throughout the liturgical year, and thus offer many more occasions for performance.

For about six centuries the term "Mass," used in musical context, has referred to a work comprising the five sung components of the Ordinary, as listed above. The choice and grouping of these texts for musical purposes was probably gradual and, to a certain extent, arbitrary; but the unit they came to constitute was a principal preoccupation of composers throughout the polyphonic period, and, less frequently, to our own time. The greatest works of earlier masters like Dufay, Dunstable, Josquin, Victoria, Palestrina, and countless others were liturgical polyphonic settings of the Ordinary of the Mass; and the finest composers of later years, men like Bach, Haydn, Mozart, Beethoven, Schubert, and Bruckner, to name but a few, have left wonderful Masses, which, while not liturgically appropriate by present standards, are magnificent art works inspired by the spirit of the traditional liturgy.

The period from approximately 1430 until the beginning of the Protestant Reformation in 1517 saw a quickening of religious fervor, and a consequent renewal of interest in writing sacred music. The majority of musicians, in the later part of this period especially, were of Low Country origin, and are generally referred to collectively as the Flemish School. They were not only tremendously energetic and prolific in their musical activities, but they were great travelers. As a result, scarcely a country or a court of Europe failed to feel their influence. Most of the important musical forms of the High Renaissance were of Flemish origin or were developed and perfected by these tireless Lowlanders; thus the polyphonic Mass and motet, Italian madrigal, French chanson, and various early instrumental forms are all basically Flemish-inspired. Ockeghem, Josquin, and Willaert, in particular, were great teachers, and were thus the founders of musical tradition for at least two generations to come.

Of the group of Flemish composers who flourished in the quarter century before the onset of the Protestant Reformation, few were more active or of wider influence than Heinrich Isaac. The exact place and date of his birth are uncertain, but he was probably born somewhere in the Low Countries about 1450.[4] He is known to have worked at the Court of Ferrara around 1480, and somewhat later he served Lorenzo the Magnificent (1449–1492) in Florence, as court composer and music tutor to Lorenzo's children. His activity there apparently terminated with the collapse of Medici prestige in Florence, after Lorenzo's death in 1492. Some time later, probably about 1500, he commenced service as chief composer in the *Hofkapelle* of Kaiser Maximilian I, who was one of the greatest music and art patrons of all time. His associates and pupils while he held this post were some of the greatest musicians of the day, men of diverse nationalities and outstanding talent. He was at liberty, moreover, to travel freely. Isaac was apparently an extraordinarily perceptive and impressionable person, for he absorbed all the variety and color of his many environments, and developed what has been described as the first "international" style. He retired from Maximilian's service in 1514, with honor and a generous pension, and returned to Florence, where he died in 1517.

Although Isaac has written in a variety of forms, sacred and secular, and for both choral and instrumental mediums, his liturgical works are unquestionably his most serious and significant, as well as the most numerous. He is known to

[1] At High Mass; at Low Mass all texts are spoken in a low voice by the celebrant at the altar.

[2] Except Sundays after Easter and a few other occasions.

[3] After the Council of Trent in the mid-sixteenth century, only four sequences remained, a fifth being added later: those for the feasts of Easter (*Victimae paschali laudes*), Pentecost (*Veni, sancte Spiritus*), Corpus Christi (*Lauda, Sion*), and the Seven Sorrows of the Blessed Virgin Mary (*Stabat Mater*) (this last an eighteenth-century addition), along with the *Dies Irae* from the Proper of the Requiem Mass.

[4] See Louise Cuyler, *Choralis Constantinus, Book III* (Ann Arbor, Michigan: University of Michigan Press, 1950), pp. 8–9.

have composed at least twenty-three settings of the Ordinary of the Mass.[5] His largest and most important work is the *Choralis Constantinus*, a monumental series of motets, probably written between 1505 and 1510 for the diocese of Constance. It contains music suitable for practically every principal occasion of the liturgical calendar. The greater portion of the *Choralis Constantinus*[6] comprises motet settings of texts from the Proper of the Mass, drawn from an edition of the Roman Gradual that has never been identified.[7] The final portion of the third and last book, however, contains five settings of the Ordinary. All these are of the type commonly called "alternate verse," meaning that only alternate lines or sentences from each liturgical text, commencing always with the second one, were utilized in the composed Mass. It is generally presumed that traditional plain song was used in performance for the remainder of the texts.

All five of these Masses appear in other manuscripts and publications besides the *Choralis Constantinus*. It is not known whether they were composed initially for inclusion in this monumental work, or whether they were chosen from among Isaac's many extant settings of the Ordinary by his pupil Ludwig Senfl, when he prepared the *Choralis Constantinus* for publication, about 1531. Actual publication did not take place until 1550–1555, by Formschneider of Nürnberg, and by that time the details of Senfl's editorship were lost or forgotten. Since the texts of the Proper in the earlier portions of the *Choralis Constantinus* are also set in alternate-verse style, and since this type is not used in Isaac's other Masses, it seems likely that these five Masses were indeed written especially for this, the composer's epic work.

The General Nature of the Masses

THE TRADITION of which the alternate-verse Mass is a late phase apparently has its serious beginnings in the clausula of Notre Dame composers in the thirteenth century, especially Perotin. A clausula was a section of metered polyphony based on a chant fragment inserted into a composition whose original organum was freely melismatic or less strictly metered. The initial purpose would seem to have been the imparting of variety and interest, and through the fifteenth century a similar practice of alternating familiar and imitative contrapuntal styles for successive text sections was commonplace. By Isaac's time, the increased length and complexity of Mass settings constituted a serious problem. Thus abbreviation was undoubtedly a prime motive for the occasional use of partial texts in composed Masses. That this type was thought to be valid and effective is attested by the fact that great composers like Senfl, Victoria, and Palestrina continued to make occasional use of partial texts for half a century and more after Isaac's day.

The Kyrie, Gloria, Sanctus, and Agnus Dei movements of all five Masses in the *Choralis Constantinus* show a constant pattern of text omissions. The terminology for sections (lines) in the table of text usage that follows will be employed in all subsequent discussions of the Mass movements.

Mass movement	*Lines omitted by Isaac*	*Lines set polyphonically by Isaac*
Kyrie	Kyrie 1^a	
		Kyrie 2^a
	Kyrie 3^a	
		Christe 1
	Christe 2	
		Christe 3
	Kyrie 1^b	
		Kyrie 2^b
	Kyrie 3^b	
Gloria	["Gloria in excelsis Deo" is always intoned by the celebrant.]	
	Et in terra pax	
		Laudamus
	Benedicimus	
		Adoramus
	Glorificamus	
		Gratias
	Domine Deus	
		Domine Fili
	Domine Deus, Agnus Dei	
	Qui tollis . . . miserere[8]	
		Qui tollis . . . suscipe
	Qui sedes	
		Quoniam
	Tu solus Dominus	
		Tu solus Altissimus
	Cum Sancto Spiritu Amen	
Sanctus	Sanctus 1	
		Sanctus 2
	Sanctus 3	
		Pleni
	Hosanna	
		Benedictus
	Hosanna	
Agnus Dei	Agnus 1	
		Agnus 2
	Agnus 3	

Isaac's text omissions for the Credo, however, were not equally consistent, and varied series of lines appear in the four settings (the fifth and final Mass, entitled *Confessoribus*, lacks a Credo movement altogether). The incipit, "Credo in unum

[5] See Robert Eitner, *Biographisch-bibliographisches Quellenlexikon der Musiker und Musikgelehrten der Christlichen Zeitrechnung bis zur Mitte des 19. Jahrhunderts* (Leipzig, 1899–1904), V, 249–250.

[6] See *Denkmäler der Tonkunst in Oesterreich*, ed. Guido Adler (Leipzig and Vienna, 1894–1938), V^1 and XVI^1; and Cuyler, *Choralis Constantinus, Book III*.

[7] Before the Council of Trent, in the mid-sixteenth century, most liturgical books were regional, with prominence given to local or regional saints and events. Since that time, these office books have been standardized for the whole world.

[8] Here is the single instance of the omission of two consecutive text lines.

Deum," was always intoned by the celebrant. The first Mass, called *Solemne*, uses "Visibilium omnium" as the initial text, but continues without pause to include the second line, "Et in unum Dominum." The three remaining Credo's, those of *Pascale*, *Magne Deus*, and *Martyribus*, all begin with "Et in unum Dominum." The Credo's of *Missa Solemne* and *Missa de Martyribus* are very brief, for both these polyphonic settings conclude with the line "Et homo factus est." Thus it is evident that only in *Pascale* and *Magne Deus* are the Credo's comparable to other Mass movements in the amount of text included. (In subsequent references, lines from the Credo will be designated by their initial word or phrase.)

Isaac lived and worked in a period when many different musical styles were used in Mass writing, although the most popular were the *cantus firmus*, the parody, and the freely composed types. All parts of the *Choralis Constantinus* except the four Credo's are apparently based on Gregorian *cantus firmi*. No Gregorian source for any of the Credo's has been discovered, which suggests the possibility that they were not originally included in these Masses. The prevalence of a Gregorian *cantus firmus* did not restrict the diversity of Isaac's contrapuntal usage, however, for all manner of polyphonic device enriches the music.

A group of Mass Ordinaries comprises a most useful basis for conclusions concerning stylistic trends, because conditions of text, sectionalization, length, and so on are identical and constant. A number of traits, characteristics of Isaac's sacred style, emerge from an examination of these Masses.

Cadences

The final cadence chord is most often the archaic form that lacks a third. If the third is present, it is generally in the highest voice. Section cadences use either type of arrangement, but final cadences of movements are generally established on three roots and a fifth of the modal tonic.

The penultimate chord is, variously, V, VII_6, IV, and, once, II. As in so much music of the early sixteenth century, the V–I cadence is already greatly preferred to the habitual VII_6–I of fourteenth- and fifteenth-century usage. Almost as common, however, is IV–I, especially when the cadence group is highly contrapuntal.

In multi-sectional movements, the pitch location of section cadences is varied; but the final cadence, except in instances specifically cited in the discussions to follow, is on the modal final.

The 4–3 suspension, a cadence-group cliché all during the sixteenth century, is present continually in Isaac's counterpoint.

Modality

Since all movements except the Credo's are clearly based on *cantus firmi*, the matter of modality is important, and was undoubtedly the guiding factor for the composer in matters of cadence, range, and linear contour.

The original Gregorian mode was generally transposed by use of B♭—in four instances to an unconventional level, as will be pointed out. Of the twenty-four movements included in this group of Masses, eight use Mode 1, two Mode 4, three Mode 5, three Mode 6, six Mode 8, and two (probably) Mode 12. Classified according to movements, three Kyrie's are Mode 8, two Mode 1; two Gloria's are Mode 4, two Mode 8, and one Mode 1; two Credo's are Mode 12, one Mode 1, and one Mode 8; two Sanctus's are Mode 1, two Mode 5, and one Mode 6; two Agnus Dei's are Mode 1, two Mode 6, and one Mode 5. This proportion of modal usage appears to be close to that found in the large body of plain-song repertoire.

Most analysts hold nowadays that identification of mode in polyphonic music must be made through consideration of single lines only, and not through perception of any over-all polyphonic traits. This problem, in music based on *cantus firmi*, is relatively simple, however, especially when the *cantus firmus* is of known Gregorian derivation. The polyphonic cadences serve in most instances but to confirm the mode indicated for the plain-song source in the Roman Gradual. If discrepancy exists between the ascribed mode of the chant and Isaac's cadence practice, the reason generally has to do with avoiding tritone relationships.

Contrapuntal Style

Isaac lived in the same period as Josquin, a time when the Flemish contrapuntal tradition was at its glorious height. His magnificent craft in polyphony, more than any other trait, marks Isaac as a man of Flemish origin. Every musical ruse, device, and cliché common to the counterpoint of the Lowlanders may be perceived in Isaac's writing. The result is polyphony of the greatest freedom, variety, and inventiveness, especially as regards rhythm.

Of the five Masses that comprise the present set, the first three, *Solemne*, *Pascale*, and *Magne Deus*, are much more complex and imposing than *Martyribus* and *Confessoribus*. This fact is not surprising, since these three are clearly intended for liturgical occasions of the greatest solemnity and importance. The feasts of martyrs and confessors, except for those of apostles and a few others, are not high in the hierarchy of liturgical precedence, and so suggest simpler music.

Among the Mass movements, certain sections of the Gloria (especially the words "Jesu Christe") and the Sanctus are the most consistently impressive or florid. Kyrie 2b is likely to be rhythmically complex, and the single section of the Agnus Dei to be simple and tender. The Credo's stand alone stylistically, for they are primarily syllabic and devoid of contrapuntal device, are apparently not based on *cantus firmi*, and are remarkably straightforward and consistent in matters such as cadence, rhythm, and even notation.

In *cantus firmus* movements, the plain song is employed with all the accustomed Flemish cunning. Often the *cantus firmus* is cast in long values, continuing thus throughout a section in the chosen voice part. Almost as often, the chant is a vagrant, wandering from part to part. Most often of all, the opening motive of the plain-song source becomes the subject of initial imitation. Once the required voice entries are achieved, a single voice may continue the *cantus firmus*, or, not infrequently, the subsequent counterpoint is freely conceived and makes no further allusion to the chant source. In one case a plain-song fragment becomes a cyclic motive, which unifies the later portions of the Mass in which it is used.

Sections are variously imitative or familiar in style, often with an obviously studied attempt to achieve variety. Clearly, movements with minimal texts (Kyrie, Agnus Dei) provide the most natural opportunity for both imitative and florid writing; and "wordy" portions (Credo and Gloria) suggest use of the familiar style, to permit clear enunciation of texts and to curtail the length.

Characteristics of Individual Voices

The discant is often the *cantus firmus* voice, a role that is somewhat restrictive. Even when this voice is independent, however, it is perhaps the least bold and interesting of the four, and is likely to carry notes of long duration as a foil for floridity beneath, in the other parts. It often enters late in an imitative series, or achieves the cadence tone several breves in advance of the rest of the counterpoint.

The alto is the most consistently florid of all the parts, and, more often than not, fails to participate in imitation. Typically, the alto is a vagrant, independent, complementary voice of peripatetic tendencies, which is kept ready to accomplish such musical chores as filling in missing notes, quickening the rhythmic movement, or reiterating important text. As a whole, it is virtually equal-voiced with the tenor, and could be effectively sung only by a male alto of high accomplishment. Isaac's alto parts are of the sort that has suggested instrumental realization to many scholars.

The tenor is still, as in earlier times, the heart of the counterpoint. To this part are commonly assigned contrapuntal plums, such as dramatic points of entry, important suspensions, and the like. The *cantus firmus* does not habitually lodge in the tenor, except in imitation. Isaac's most effective and individual usage pairs tenor and bass, in a fashion foreshadowing Monteverdi. These duos usually commence a section and often persist for a distance of several breves before the higher parts enter at all.

The bass is consistently bold, free, widespread, and, at cadences, downright "harmonic." At important closing points, the bass commonly carries the root of the penultimate harmony (IV or V) and resolves it to the modal tonic. The bass often carries the *cantus firmus*, is frequently melismatic, and, as a whole, is Isaac's most exciting part, for it is completely varied, unpredictable, and uninhibited.

Rhythmic Aspects

Time signatures are, variously, **C**, **¢**, **O**, **Φ**, and proportions of all of these. Isaac worked in that intermediate period when the meaning of *alla breve*, in particular, appears to have been inconsistent, ambiguous, or both. In the present transcriptions, therefore, **¢** and **Φ** are transcribed according to context, sometimes as a doubling of the tempo (diminution), often as merely indication of an *accelerando*, with no change of unit value. The interpretation of each *alla breve* is indicated in the discussions to follow.

Another rhythmic problem, one that is a commonplace in early sixteenth-century music, pertains to the more intricate prolations in *tempus perfectum* (**O** or **Φ**). In these meters, the minima groups fall naturally into larger units of two or three, in free alternation. Older transcriptional practice changed the modern time signature back and forth between $\frac{3}{2}$ and $\frac{6}{4}$, according to the grouping of the moment, but this was often complicated and confusing. Where the problem exists in these Mass transcriptions a co-signature of $\frac{3}{2}\ \frac{6}{4}$ is placed at the outset of the section, a procedure that implies that the two rhythmic groupings will be found alternately in the music that follows.

Whether or not to use bar lines in modern editions of older music is almost always a troublesome question. Their presence is unquestionably of visual aid in reading, and serves to make the music readily comprehensible to those performers who are unversed in earlier notation. The danger lies in overlooking the fact that their use must never be construed as indicating the rhythmic stress so often implicit in modern usage. Bar lines are used in the present transcriptions because their advantages seem to outweigh their hazards.

Original rhythmic values have been halved in the transcriptions, so that a perfect breve yields one modern measure of $\frac{3}{2}$ time, an imperfect breve one measure of $\frac{2}{2}$. The *alla breve*, where it was interpreted as a full diminution, has been transcribed using two original breves to the modern $\frac{3}{2}$ or $\frac{2}{2}$ measure. Where it was interpreted only as *accelerando*, no notational change was made.

Texts

Most of the text of the Ordinary of the Mass had achieved constant form long before Isaac's day, although the Credo continued to suffer deletions and manipulations.[9] Thus no problem of deciphering or word identification exists, although spelling and syllabic division in the source are inconsistent and casual. In the transcriptions, the spelling and syllabification of the Latin follow the modern Roman Gradual.

The tropes, which will be cited in the discussions of separate movements, are archaisms, but were not uncommon in the sixteenth century. "Marian" tropes, in particular, persisted into the next century; and despite continued efforts at canonical restraint, these extra texts remained a favorite device, one to use in connection with names of dramatic import like "Jesu Christe," "Dominus," and "Maria," especially.

The problem of word underlaying is a troublesome matter in most sixteenth-century music, and these Masses are no exceptions. Often musical motives are so shaped that the appropriate text word is unmistakable. More often, however, especially in the sparse texts of the Kyrie or the Sanctus, melismatic passages occur for which only three solutions are evident: constant text repetition; use of a long melisma on a mid-syllable with a deliberate deferment of the final syllable to the close of the melodic figure; or simply a "wordless melisma," which medieval writers had often indicated as the epitome of jubilation.

Since conclusive information concerning contemporary performance practices is lacking, the word underlaying in these transcriptions has been made as vocal as possible, and observes any known traditions of Isaac's day.

Notation

The *Choralis Constantinus* is commonly cited as containing the most devious, involved, and deliberately cryptic notation of the music of the entire Flemish period. Whether these esoteric notational procedures were a form of intellectual-mathematical virtuosity, or whether they were a deliberate attempt to restrict performance to the initiate members of the musical cult is not clear. Whatever the motive, the difficulty of deciphering and transcribing much of the Flemish music of this period has undoubtedly been a major factor in

---

9 See Ruth Hannas, "Concerning Deletions in the Polyphonic Mass Credo," *Journal of the American Musicological Society*, V (1952), 155–186.

discouraging its appearance in modern editions. Every ruse of proportion, coloration, ligature, and the like is used, and transcription of the music might be better sport for a fan of the double acrostic than for a musician.

The character of these Masses makes them liturgically useful even now, and within the strictest reading of the 1903 *Motu Proprio* concerning sacred music for the Roman liturgy. If performance were to be undertaken, the omitted texts should be interpolated and sung in the plain-song setting of the source from which the polyphony derived its *cantus firmus*. To this end, the plain-song source, if known, has been indicated in the detailed discussions of the separate Mass movements that follow.

The Separate Movements of the Masses[10]

I. *MISSA SOLEMNE*

KYRIE

Source of *CF*: *GR* Mass IV, *In Festis Duplicibus* 1, [11] (*Cunctipotens Genitor Deus*).

Mode: 1 transposed.[12]

Sections

Kyrie 2a.—O.

The discant has the *CF*, basically in full breves, but with some diversity through passing tones at cadence approaches. The other three parts co-operate in three-voiced, nonimitative counterpoint, independent of the *CF*. Cadence is V–I in G.

Christe 1.—O2, transcribed diminution.

Same style and cadence as Kyrie 2a.

Christe 3.—¢, transcribed diminution.

The change to imperfect time makes this trio section sound bolder and more vigorous, although the tenor is tacet. The *CF* is still in the discant, but is not continuous, since freely derived motives are interpolated throughout. The alto and bass are often imitative of each other. Cadence is V–I in G.

Kyrie 2b.—Φ, transcribed diminution.

The *CF* is in the discant, but is freely varied after the first six notes. The tenor and bass are partly imitative, while the alto is independent. This section is the most florid of the movement, and cadences V–I in G.

GLORIA

Source of *CF*: *GR* Mass IV.

Mode: 4 transposed.

Sections

Laudamus.—O.

The *CF*, slightly varied from the modern version, appears in breves in two voices: the discant and simultaneously, in retrograde, the tenor. Alto and bass, which are independent and florid, accomplish V–I in D by linear means, surrounding the slower-moving discant and tenor.

Adoramus.—C.

The *CF* appears in imperfect breves in the discant. Alto and tenor state a free contrapuntal associate in unusual perfect canon at the unison. The bass is boldly harmonic, vigorous, and spaced in wide intervals. The harmonic cadence is IV–I in D, but the canonic voices suggest a linear authentic cadence in their extension.

Gratias.—O2, transcribed diminution.

The *CF* comprises the first eleven notes of the bass, imitated at the fifth one measure later in the tenor. From the word "propter," both parts are free of the *CF* and melismatic. Discant and alto are independent and florid throughout the section, which cadences IV–I in D.

Domine Fili.—Φ, transcribed diminution.

The *CF*, almost unrecognizable through rhythmic mutation and ornamental tones, appears in the discant. All four voices are florid and mostly independent of each other, although there is some brief motivic imitation. The cadence, achieved linearly, is IV–I in A. This is the Gloria's first close on the final of the transposed Hypophrygian mode, and is especially forceful after the three preceding cadences on the transposed modal dominant, D.

The troped word "Altissime" is added at the close of the regular liturgical text, and underlines the broad plagal cadence.

Qui tollis . . . suscipe.—¢, transcribed without diminution.

The *CF* is dispersed in breves among the discant, tenor, and bass voices. The alto is free, and there is sporadic imitation of motives throughout the section. Of especially potent effect in achieving the rare mid-section cadence with fermata, V–I in B♭ at the text "suscipe," is the withholding of the bass entry until almost that point. The final section cadence is again V–I in D.

Quoniam.—¢3, transcribed without diminution.

The contrapuntal style and cadence resemble those of the preceding section.

Tu solus Altissimus.—¢, transcribed without diminution.

Only in the opening breves in the tenor is allusion made to the *CF*. All of the parts are boldly written, and are interrupted often by rests, which have a most invigorating effect. At the final text, "Jesu Christe," there occurs a very striking passage, characterized by intricate rhythmic relationships among all the parts, and an especially vigorous bass. The cadence IV–I in A is achieved linearly by the alto and bass while the discant and tenor sustain an octave A for five breves' duration.

CREDO

Source of *CF*: Lacking.

Mode: 1 transposed.

Sections

Visibilium.—O.

The four voices enter successively, bass, alto, tenor, dis-

[10] Throughout the discussion that follows, *CF* stands for *cantus firmus* and *GR* for *Graduale Romanum*. The plain-song source of the *cantus firmus* is given in the Appendix if it is known.

[11] The sources are numbered and titled as in modern editions of *GR*.

[12] The number of the mode is that indicated for the plain song in *GR*, if this source was known. If B♭ appears in the signature, the mode is designated "transposed."

cant, on a strong yet simple motive that provides syllabic treatment for the first text word, "visibilium." The imitation is exact through only the first breve value, and is actually merely a device whereby the voices are set into motion. As the section proceeds, other brief points of imitation occur, most often between discant and alto. The cadence is a plagal in G.

Deum de Deo.—O2, transcribed diminution.
The discant and alto enter first, with two complementary motives; tenor and bass follow two breves later, in free imitation of the dux parts. Cadence is V–I in G.

Per quem.—₵, transcribed without diminution.
This section is relatively simple, with brief points of imitation throughout. The meter becomes perfect at "et propter," a change that, as usual, tends to facilitate movement. The cadence is V–I in G.

Ex Maria.—₵, transcribed without diminution.
The text is set in free counterpoint through "Virgine." "Et homo factus est," as is traditional, is set in more serious and impressive style. While the discant of this section continues to be written **C**, the remaining voices are notated proportionately with the signature **O**. The opening motive is the descending position of a major triad, which enters simultaneously in the discant and in the tenor, written in a $\frac{3}{4}$ proportionate augmentation. The alto enters one breve later, carries imitation only through the triadal motive, then proceeds freely. The bass enters last, with imitation of the triadal motive a fifth lower, followed by a free part. Cadence is V–I in G.

This very brief setting of the Credo differs from other movements of this Mass in its contrapuntal style, which is free rather than *CF*-based, and in its consistent, strongly harmonic section cadences in G, final of transposed Mode 1.

SANCTUS

Source of *CF*: Lacking except as noted below.

Mode: 1 transposed.

Sections

Sanctus 2.—₵, transcribed without diminution.
Although the chant source is unknown, the nine-note ligature in the tenor is clearly treated as the *CF*. Since the two remaining sections of this Sanctus (the Pleni and the Benedictus) use the opening four-note motive of the Agnus of this same *Missa Solemne* as *CF* motive, it appears probable that these two final movements were planned cyclically on a common motive whose Gregorian source is that given for the Agnus Dei. Bass and discant are partly imitative, but the alto is free, and the section cadence is plagal in G.

Pleni.—O2, transcribed diminution.
The borrowed *CF* (see above) commences in the tenor, but is apparently used through only the first four notes. The movement is unusually free and florid in all parts, closing with an authentic cadence in G.

Benedictus.—₵, transcribed without diminution.
The borrowed *CF* motive is used for imitation at the opening, in discant and tenor voices. No other allusion to the *CF* is made, although the tenor at "qui" has a five-note ligature that resembles a chant fragment. The movement is characterized by extensive use of sequence, both in successive motives within the same part, and in the commoner inter-voice imitations. The cadence is V–I in G.

AGNUS DEI

Source of *CF*: GR Mass II, *In Festis Solemnibus* 1.

Mode: 1 transposed.

Section

Agnus 2.—₵, transcribed without diminution.
In this movement the four-note *CF* motive is in its proper liturgical context, and recurs throughout, first in imitation between discant and tenor, and sporadically in other voices. Alto and bass have imitation of a contrapuntal associate at the beginning. This pairing of voices in double imitation is a favorite technique among the early group of Flemish composers. The cadence is V–I of G.

II. *MISSA PASCALE*

KYRIE

Source of *CF*: GR Mass I, *Tempore Paschali* (*Lux et Origo*).

Mode: 8 transposed.

Sections

Kyrie 2a.—O (Φ in tenor is an obvious error).
The *CF* appears first as a five-note motive, in octave imitation among bass, tenor, and discant. The bass then has a fourth statement of the *CF* fragment a perfect fourth higher than initially. The word "eleison" in the tenor underlies the second chant motive, in a figure which elides with the final breve of the *CF* motive in the bass. The alto is free throughout, as are the other parts except when they have the *CF*. The cadence is a plagal in D, supertonic of transposed Mode 8.

Christe 1.—₵, transcribed diminution (signature omitted in the source).
CF enters as a nine-note motive, treated imitatively in four successive entries in alto, bass, tenor, and discant. The first imitation, in the bass, is at the perfect fourth below, but the other two are at the octave. The second chant fragment, "eleison," appears in imitation between soprano and tenor. The counterpoint is simple, except in the triplets of the last eight breves before the authentic cadence in C, the mode final.

Christe 3.—₵, transcribed diminution.
This three-voiced section with tenor tacet is free of the *CF* except for the initial three-note motive, which introduces imitative entries in bass, alto, and discant. Cadence is V–I in C.

Kyrie 2b.—Φ, transcribed diminution.
Four notes of the *CF* are the subject of the opening imitation in bass, tenor, discant, and finally alto. Four more notes of the *CF* are treated imitatively in tenor and alto only. Cadence is V–I in C.

GLORIA

Source of *CF*: *GR* Mass I.

Mode: 4 transposed.

Sections

Laudamus.—¢, transcribed without diminution throughout this Gloria.

The *CF* occurs in breves in the discant with a variation from the modern *GR* in the presence of one extra note, the third. The remaining voices have simple counterpoint, principally in familiar style. Cadence is V–I in D, the modal dominant.

Adoramus.—¢.

The style of the Laudamus continues, but cadence is V–I in C, the mediant of the mode.

Gratias.—¢.

The *CF* again appears, slightly varied from *GR*, in breves in the discant, while the alto and tenor voices carry a countersubject in imitation spaced at the unusual distance of six breves. The bass, which commences one semibreve after the discant, is boldly harmonic, and comprises terse four- or five-note motives, punctuated by rests. A mid-section cadence, V–I in C, marked by a fermata, occurs at "tibi." The final cadence, also in C, is harmonically indeterminate, since voice relationships remain fluid until the final breve in the discant is reached. The general illusion, created by the active tones in all voices in the area of the cadence approach, is that a plagal cadence is implied.

Domine Fili.—¢.

Voices are paired in this section, with the bass and the tenor proceeding a distance of fourteen breves before the alto and the discant, also paired, enter. The *CF*, freely treated, appears in the tenor, with only a florid bass associate, until entry of the upper voices at "Jesu." From here the *CF* moves from alto to bass, and back to the alto at the cadence, V–I in C.

Qui tollis . . . suscipe.—¢.

Again the *CF* is a vagrant part, commencing in the discant to "mundi," moving to the bass for the single word "suscipe," and to the alto for "deprecationem nostram." The text underlaying is unmistakable here, because of the frequent vivid punctuation of rests and one fermata, at "suscipe." The bass voice does not enter at all until "suscipe," a word whose three syllables are stressed by this first achieving of full four-part harmony, as well as by use of a full breve in all parts for each syllable. The cadence is VII_6–I in C, a progression that was a near cliché among Burgundian composers of the fifteenth century, but that had probably begun to sound a little archaic by Isaac's time.

Quoniam.—¢.

The whole treatment of this section is involved, especially through inter-voice rhythmic relationships. The tenor, a very free usage of the *CF*, is cast in a complicated rhythmic pattern that is dispersed over a three-breve valuation. This pattern is repeated five times in exact rhythmic sequence, but with melodic variation. The other voices have counterpoint that is varied and only sporadically imitative. Hemiola, notated in blackened triplet groups, covers the last three breves of valuation. The cadence is IV–I in D.

Tu solus Altissimus.—¢.

Voices are paired for entries in double imitation: the *CF* in bass with countersubject in alto, the *CF* in tenor with countersubject in discant. At "Jesu Christe," the *CF* is subject to imitation in alto, bass, and then tenor parts, while the discant maintains independent counterpoint up to the cadence group. The close of this final polyphonic section is a powerful V–I in C.

A significant feature of Isaac's setting of this Gloria is that no cadence occurs on the final of transposed Mode 4, A. There are two cadences on the modal dominant, D, and five on the mediant, C.

CREDO

Source of *CF*: Lacking.

Mode: 12 (Ionian) transposed.[13]

Sections

Et in unum.—¢, transcribed without diminution throughout this Credo.

This opening section is distinctive by reason of the proportions among the three upper voices in their statements of an identical triadal motive. All three voices commence simultaneously and use this motive at the outset; but the tenor is a diminution of the discant, while the alto, in turn, is a diminution of the tenor. Thus the same melodic figure occurs in breves, semibreves, and minimas, in the discant, tenor, and alto parts, respectively. The bass enters later than the other voices, and is freely florid, as are all the parts once the opening proportions are achieved. The cadence is V–I in F, the final of transposed Ionian mode.

Qui propter.—¢.

The writing is simple, with a consistent use of paired voices. Cadence is V–I in F.

Ex Maria.—¢.

This text, through "homo factus est," is impressively set in full breves in all parts. Cadence is IV–I in D.

Et resurrexit.—¢.

The section commences on imitation of a simple motive, with successive entries in each of the four parts. Cadence is V–I in F.

Cujus regni.—¢.

The musical treatment is similar to that of the preceding section, with a cadence IV–I in F.

Confiteor.—¢.

The remainder of the Credo text, three segments commencing "Confiteor," "Et expecto," and "Et vitam," in addition to the final "Amen," are given continuous polyphonic treatment with no omissions. This proce-

[13] Though Glarean's definite codification of the twelve modes in the *Dodekachordon* did not appear until 1547, some forty years after Isaac's work was probably written, practical use of the newer ninth, tenth, eleventh, and twelfth modes was commonplace by the early sixteenth century.

dure is graphic illustration of the remark made earlier, that the settings of the Credo pursue no consistent, orderly plan of text omission. The final cadence is again IV–I in F.

As a whole, this Credo is one of Isaac's simplest movements. The counterpoint is in the routine cliché style of the day; and the constant use both of *alla breve* time and of the mode that corresponds to the modern major scale (Ionian) tends to make the Credo sound rather commonplace. This movement clearly exemplifies the traits of style that further the opinion that the four Credo movements were not present in the original versions of these Masses.

SANCTUS

Source of *CF: GR* Mass XVII, *In Dominicis Adventus et Quadragesimae.*

Mode: 5.[14]

Sections

Sanctus 2.—Ͻ and ⌽, transcribed diminution.

This section is one of the most complicated in the entire group of Masses. The time signatures indicate interpart proportions of great complexity, since the discant carries Ͻ, while the remaining three parts have ⌽. The *CF* appears in discant breves of "half-coloration" ◧, which yield five-partite durations in modern notation. The result is, obviously, a constant shift of rhythmic stress, since the change of note occurs always at a different point within the *integer valor.* The three lower voices, meanwhile, pursue the most intricate imitative polyphony. The cadence is VII_6–I in C, approached in a very florid manner in the three lower parts. This section is clear proof of Isaac's Flemish origin.

Pleni.—C in discant, ¢ in bass, signature lacking in alto and tenor; transcribed without diminution.

This portion is much simpler than Sanctus 2, with the *CF* in broad values in the discant, a simple counterpoint stated imitatively in alto and bass, and the tenor tacet. The cadence is vertically ambiguous, but is achieved by linear activity in alto and bass, beneath an inverted pedal C of five breves' duration in the discant. The final close is C, which continues the modal ambiguity of Sanctus 2.

Benedictus.—O2, transcribed diminution.

The complicated style of Sanctus 2 returns in this section, with the *CF* again in discant, now alternately in white and colored longas (breves by the signature diminution), which are transcribed as notes of six-partite and five-partite duration, respectively. The other three parts pursue their own involved counterpoint, frequently in imitative fragments. This section has the only strong, vertical cadence of the movement, V–I in C, the effect of which is heightened by a sudden shift to imperfect time for the closing group.

AGNUS DEI

Source of *CF: GR* Mass XVII.

Mode: 5 (see footnote 14).

Sections

Agnus 2.—C.

The first seven notes of the *CF* appear, with ornamentation, in the alto, which voice rarely carries the chant line. After this brief allusion to the plain song, the parts are contrapuntally independent through to the plagal cadence in F that closes the section.

III. *MISSA MAGNE DEUS*

KYRIE

Source of *CF: GR* Mass V, *In Festis Duplicibus* 2 (*Kyrie Magnae Deus Potentiae*).

Mode: 8 transposed.

Sections

Kyrie 2a.—O.

The *CF* appears first in the discant, then, imitatively, in the tenor. The initial lines in both alto and bass are *CF*-derived, but move freely after five notes. The principal section cadence is V–I in C, although the illusion of a plagal post-cadence follows in the active lines of alto and bass, which surround the sustained notes C of discant and tenor.

Christe 1.—C.

A six-note chant motive is the subject of opening imitation in all parts, after which the section moves in simple polyphony to a strongly harmonic V–I cadence in C.

Christe 3.—¢, transcribed diminution.

The discant is tacet, but the entire Gregorian *CF* appears in the tenor, written in free rhythm. There is no real imitation, although the alto line at the start is derived melodically from the *CF.* The bass is free, and all voices participate in the VII_6–I close in C.

Kyrie 2b.—¢3, transcribed diminution.

A five-note motive from the *CF* serves as subject of an imitative opening, which includes all four voices. The discant, last to enter, continues the *CF* to the cadence area. Here there occurs, first, a V–I close, then a plagal post-cadence in C, thus duplicating the cadence procedure of Kyrie 2a.

GLORIA.

Source of *CF: GR Cantus ad Libitum, Gloria* I.

Mode: 8 transposed.

Sections

Laudamus.—O.

The *CF* occurs in breves in the discant, while the other parts proceed in simple counterpoint to a V–I close in C.

Adoramus.—¢, transcribed diminution throughout this Gloria.

[14] GR labels this Sanctus and the Agnus Dei that follows, Mode 5. In neither does Isaac transpose the notes, although he does use B♭ in the signature, as was his practice in transposition. In the Sanctus, the effect, since all section cadences are in C, is close to that of transposed Mode 7—Mixolydian—or possibly Mode 12—Ionian. The one cadence of the Agnus Dei is a plagal in F, so that the effect is closer to that of Mode 12.

Again the *CF* appears in the discant, with imitation of the first four notes in the tenor, and free parts in alto and bass. Cadence is VII_6–I in C, with a light plagal post-cadence.

Gratias.—₵.

A six-note chant motive is used for initial imitation between alto and bass. Thereafter only the bass alludes, intermittently, to the plain song, and all parts move to a V–I close in C.

Domine Fili.—₵.

The bass carries the *CF* through "unigenite." Alto and tenor parts are *CF*-derived through their first three notes, but the discant is entirely free. The troped words "et Sancte Spiritus" are added after the liturgical text at "Jesu Christe." There follows a strong authentic cadence in C.

Qui Tollis . . . suscipe.—₵.

The *CF* is carried alternately by bass and tenor, while the other parts pursue free contrapuntal associates. The cadence is V–I in G.

Quoniam.—₵ (signature omitted in the source—in this and similar instances, a signature is assumed from the context).

Bass and tenor pair for imitation of a free version of the *CF*, while alto and discant combine for imitative treatment of a contrapuntal associate. The cadence is as curious and inconclusive as any in these Masses. The real close is achieved in G, through a penultimate harmony of the triad F A C in root position. The usual *musica ficta* F♯ cannot be supplied in the bass, because the tenor also has the note F in a context that makes alteration improbable in this style. While alto and bass sustain G, the discant has a semibreve rest and resumes the chord-third, B, afterward. The tenor has a neighboring tone E that suggests a plagal post-cadence.

Tu solus Altissimus.—₵ (signature omitted in the source). The entire *CF* appears with little variation in the tenor, and with imitation in the bass through the first half of the chant line. Alto and discant commence imitatively with an associate part, but soon become free of each other. The final cadence is a plagal in C, the final of the mode.

CREDO

Source of *CF*: Lacking.

Mode: 12 (Ionian).

Sections

Et in unum.—₵, transcribed without diminution throughout this Credo.

As is true in the two preceding Credo's, the counterpoint appears to be free, and not *CF*-based. After paired imitation through two motives, the parts pursue their uncomplicated way to an authentic cadence in C.

Genitum—₵.

The section is without complication, and achieves a weak (incomplete) VII_6–I in C.

Ex Maria—Φ, then ₵.

This section exhibits a little more contrapuntal resource than most parts of the Credo's. "Virgine" is marked by a mid-section cadence, VII_6–I in G, and a fermata. The time changes to imperfect for "Et homo factus est," and this, like any metric change, serves to emphasize these words, the most solemn of the Credo. The final section close is VII_6–I in C.

Et resurrexit.—₵.

The section is uncomplicated, proceeding to a V–I close in C.

Et in Spiritum.—₵.

This simple duo for alto and bass is only casually imitative, and closes in an implied VII_6–I cadence in C.

Et in unam sanctam catholicam.—₵3, then ₵.

This section alternates familiar with imitative style, and duple with triple time. The movement cadence is V–I in C.

SANCTUS

Source of *CF*: *GR* Mass II, *In Festis Solemnibus* 1.

Mode: 1 transposed.

Sections

Sanctus 2.—Φ, transcribed without diminution.

The *CF* is stated in breves in the discant, and simultaneously in retrograde in the tenor. Alto and bass parts are contrapuntally free, and are the means of achieving a plagal close in G, while discant and tenor sustain an octave of the modal final, G.

Pleni.—₵, transcribed without diminution.

All four voices partake sporadically in imitation of the *CF* line. The alto has diminution of the *CF* through five semibreves, then is contrapuntally free. The cadence is VII_6–I in D.

Benedictus.—₵, transcribed without diminution.

The *CF* is a vagrant voice that moves freely from part to part. Several fresh points of imitation occur during the course of the section, and the cadence again is VII_6–I in D, the dominant of transposed Dorian mode. It is apparent that only Sanctus 2 of the three sections of this movement cadences on the modal final, G. This circumstance, while it is perhaps conspicuous in Mode 1, is not musically determinative, since the twice-omitted "Hosanna in excelsis," probably sung in the plain song of the Gregorian source, would follow both Pleni and Benedictus sections in actual performance.

AGNUS DEI

Source of *CF*: *GR* Mass XV, *In Festis Simplicibus.*

Mode: 1 transposed.

Section

Agnus 2.—C.

Tenor and discant commence with imitation of the distinctive *CF* motive. Although the *CF* of this Agnus and that of the Sanctus which precedes it are not derived from the same Gregorian Mass, an affinity is suggested by the strong opening interval of a rising perfect fifth, which characterizes the *CF* of each movement. The counterpoint is moderately florid, and the cadence is V–I in G.

IV. MISSA DE MARTYRIBUS

KYRIE

Source of *CF*: *GR* Mass XI, *In Dominicis Infra Annum (Orbis Factor)*.

Mode: 1 transposed.

Sections

Kyrie 2a.—C.

Six notes of the *CF* are the subject of initial imitation in the four voices. The remainder of the chant line, slightly altered, appears in the discant, while the tenor and the bass have counterpoint based on the initial motive. The alto is free, once the opening imitation is accomplished. Cadence is IV–I in D.

Christe 1.—¢, transcribed without diminution.

The *CF* appears in the tenor, mostly in full breves. Bass and discant, which commence imitatively, complete the counterpoint of this section, for the alto is tacet. Cadence is IV–I in D.

Christe 3.—¢, transcribed without diminution.

This duo between alto and bass uses a free version of the *CF* for imitation that is close to being exact canon. The cadence is ambiguous harmonically, but gives the illusion of VII_6–I in A.

Kyrie 2b.—¢, transcribed without diminution.

The *CF* is treated in three-voice imitation at the start, while the discant, commencing simultaneously with the last imitative entry in the tenor, is free. Alto and bass begin their imitation simultaneously, which is possible through the fact that the alto is diminution of the bass. The rhythm is kept lively throughout because the hemiola measure alternates constantly with simple *alla breve*. The cadence is IV–I in A.

The cadence structure of this Kyrie is unusual, because there are no V–I cadences, and because none of the four cadences centers on the final of transposed Mode 1: G.

GLORIA

Source of *CF*: *GR* Mass II, *In Festis Solemnibus* 1.

Mode: 1 transposed.[15]

Sections

Laudamus.—O.

The *CF*, lacking the third note as in *GR*, appears in the discant, and is complemented with as simple counterpoint as possible in the other voices. Cadence is IV–I in A.

Adoramus.—C.

Voices are paired to carry, in each case, the *CF* and a contrapuntal associate. The *CF* is first in the tenor, its imitation in the discant. Cadence is again IV–I in A.

Gratias.—¢, transcribed without diminution throughout this Gloria.

The stepwise motive, which is used in the imitative beginning, comprises the first three notes of the *CF*, with a filling-in of the first interval of a fourth. A much ornamented and manipulated version of the chant continues in the discant through "agimus tibi." At "propter," the *CF* transfers to long breves in the tenor, but returns to the discant at "gloriam," and becomes virtually imperceptible in the cadence group, which achieves a plagal close in D. Although the section is relatively simple, it is characterized by considerable contrapuntal device and ingenuity, like the diminution of the opening motive when it is taken by alto and discant.

Domine Fili.—¢.

The *CF* is assigned to the tenor throughout, and often differs considerably from the chant as shown in *GR*. Bass and alto commence with imitation of a contrapuntal associate, but proceed freely after three notes. The entrance of the discant is delayed to concur with the insertion of the extra (troped) text, "salus nostra," which precedes the final words of the section, "Jesu Christe." The music for these four closing words is broad and impressive, concluding with another plagal cadence in D.

Qui tollis . . . suscipe.—¢.

The *CF* is the subject of imitation, at the start, between tenor and discant, and the chant, freely ornamented, continues in the tenor throughout the section. A second point of imitation, this time comprising all four voices, occurs at "suscipe," after a mid-section cadence IV–I in A, with fermata. Two notable features of this section are the remarkably bold, widely spaced bass line in the beginning, and the unusual VII_6–I cadence in A at the close, which uses a minor triad, third in the bass, as penultimate, thus creating a slight illusion of Phrygian mode.

Quoniam.—¢.

The *CF* is in discant throughout, and the tenor is tacet for this trio. The bass and the alto pursue imitation of a contrapuntal associate, which is itself notable because of the melodic sequence it contains. Cadence is the rare II–I in A.

Tu solus Altissimus.—¢.

The *CF*, in bass and, occasionally, in discant, is imperceptible until "Altissimus," although the diatonic motive of opening imitation between bass and alto might be interpreted as a free filling-in of the chant line. The broad and vigorous counterpoint at "Jesu Christe" concludes in a florid plagal cadence on A.

This Gloria is notable in its unusual transposition (see footnote 15), and in its lack of any of the usual V–I or VII_6–I (usual version) cadences, so frequent in most other movements.

CREDO

Source of *CF*: Lacking.

Mode: 8 transposed.

[15] Isaac's transposition in this movement is not a fourth higher, as is conventional when one flat is used, but a fifth higher. His cadences are consistent with the transposition of the *CF*, for five out of seven section cadences are in A, not G, the final of transposed Mode 1. The effect produced is that of Mode 3 or 4. The same transposition occurs in the Gloria and the Sanctus of *Missa de Martyribus*.

Sections

Et in unum.—**C**.

This section is mostly syllabic, and is essentially very simple. The four voices commence with imitation based on a stepwise motive, and proceed to a V–I close in C.

Qui propter.—**C**.

This section resembles the preceding one, including its cadence group.

Ex Maria.—**C** (signature omitted in the source).

As in the *Missa Solemne*, this section is the final one in the brief Credo. All voices participate in the initial imitation of a simple motive, although the discant enters nine breves late. There is no fermata or palpable separation before "et homo factus est." The cadence again is V–I in C.

SANCTUS

Source of *CF*: *GR* Mass IX, *In Festis B. Mariae Virginis* 1.

Mode: 5 transposed (see footnote 15).

Sections

Sanctus 2.—**O**.

The three notes of the *CF* appear in the discant and simultaneously, in retrograde, in the tenor. Bass and alto are freely complementary. Cadence is IV–I in A.

Pleni.—**O2**, transcribed diminution.

This section appears to have little affinity to the corresponding chant section, although the opening breves in the discant actually comprise the chant motive at "terra" in the Gregorian source. The tenor is tacet, while bass and alto are unusually florid, and sporadically imitative. Cadence is VII_6–I in A.

Benedictus.—**¢**, transcribed without diminution.

The *CF* appears briefly in the alto, but this section, like the Pleni, is mostly free of the chant source. The discant has a striking long-note part, which resembles a Gregorian line in its contours. At "in nomine" the writing grows simpler and proceeds to a clear plagal cadence in A.

AGNUS DEI

Source of *CF*: *GR* Mass IV, *In Festis Duplicibus* 1.

Mode: 6 transposed.

Section

Agnus 2.—**¢**, transcribed without diminution.

Again, as in the Agnus Dei of *Missa Pascale*, and the Gloria and Sanctus of the present Mass, Isaac has not made the transposition which was conventional when one flat appeared in the signature. The pitches are raised only a third, instead of the usual fourth, probably because the fourth in Mode 6 entails the tritone relationship (B♭–E in transposition). Thus the initial motive, which conventionally would have been B♭D E(♭) F, appears as A C D E. Immediately apparent is the fact that the characteristic melodic sound of the lower pentachord of Mode 6 is not present in this group of pitches, and that Mode 4 (Hypophrygian) is actually suggested. The section cadence, IV–I in A, bears this out. Except for the initial motive, which is introduced imitatively by bass, tenor, and then discant, there is no allusion to the chant source. The contrapuntal style is simple, with a diminution of the *CF* motive at the outset in the free alto part, and occasional imitation of simple figures thereafter.

V. *MISSA DE CONFESSORIBUS*

KYRIE

Source of *CF*: *GR* Mass XII, *In Festis Semiduplicibus* 1 (*Pater Cuncta*).

Mode: 8 transposed, but lacking signature B♭.

Sections

Kyrie 2^a.—**O**.

The first four notes of the *CF* are the subject of opening imitation between discant and tenor, and the first three notes are used also in the quasi-imitative alto and bass entries. Actually, the reference to the *CF* is so brief, and the figure involved is so commonplace, that this entire Kyrie might be plausibly judged to be freely composed, or possibly to use a *CF* that is no longer retained in the *GR*. The section cadence is V–I in C.

Christe 1.—**¢**, transcribed without diminution throughout this Kyrie.

This duo between tenor and bass employs the same diatonic motive as Kyrie 2^a and proceeds to an implied VII_6–I close in C.

Christe 3.—**¢**.

This trio, with tenor tacet, resembles Christe 1, but employs the V–I close in C.

Kyrie 2^b.—**Φ**.

No reference is made to the *CF*. The section comprises imitative entries of a simple motive in discant, alto, and bass, with the tenor free after two notes. The final cadence is, curiously, IV–I in E, which tends to vitiate Mode 8, and to mark the identification of the *CF* as even more tenuous than is indicated by the melodic usage. It must be remembered, however, that the three preceding cadences have been on the proper final for transposed Mode 8, and that Kyrie 2^b is not the close of this movement, since, in performance, it would be followed by Kyrie 3^b, probably in plain song.

GLORIA

Source of *CF*: Lacking.[16]

Mode: 8 transposed.

Sections

Laudamus.—**O**.

Brief, simple, nonimitative, with V–I close in C.

---

[16] This Gloria does not appear to be based on *cantus firmus*, although many motives resemble familiar plain-song motives. Rather, the movement seems to be constructed cyclically from two ideas: the stepwise line, seen in discant at "Laudamus," in tenor at "Gratias," in alto and discant at "Quoniam"; and the motive of the open fifth, seen in discant at "Adoramus," in bass at "unigenite Jesu" (combined with stepwise motive in discant), in discant, alto, and tenor at "Qui tollis," and in all voices at "Tu solus."

Adoramus.—₵, transcribed without diminution throughout this Gloria.

This section is bold and vigorous, through change to imperfect *alla breve* (*accelerando*) and the use of the motive of the perfect fifth in discant, which contrasts with the stepwise progression of the same part at "Laudamus." The writing is nonimitative, with another V–I close in C.

Gratias.—₵.

The stepwise motive occurs in breves in the tenor, carrying a suggestion of plain song, while alto and bass are imitative, and discant is tacet. At "tibi" the tenor takes the second of the two basic motives, that of the perfect fifth, and the parts achieve a weak plagal cadence in A.

Domine Fili.—₵.

This section commences with imitation among the three upper parts, and alludes only briefly to the two basic motives cited above. Cadence is V–I in C.

Qui tollis . . . suscipe.—₵.

The bold open fifth motive is the subject of imitation in the three upper voices at the start. The bass enters at "suscipe," just in time to help in achieving the fermata. "Deprecationem nostram," set in chordal style, closes the section at the authentic cadence in C.

Quoniam.— ₵.

In this trio, with tenor tacet, the stepwise motive occurs in imitation between alto and discant, while the bass is free. Cadence is V–I in C.

Tu solus Altissimus.—⦶.

The open fifth motive returns for opening paired entries, which are casually imitative, and involve double diminution. The bass is cast entirely in full perfect breves, which convey a sense of great dignity, at the same time that they conform to Isaac's most frequent treatment of a chant line. The cadence is V–I in C.

This Gloria as a whole is marked by its apparent lack of a plain-song basis, but its compensation lies in two cyclic motives.

SANCTUS

Source of *CF*: *GR* Mass VIII, *In Festis Duplicibus 5*.

Mode: 6 transposed, but lacking signature B♭.[17]

Sections

Sanctus 2.—O.

The second member of the four-note *CF* motive, as shown in *GR*, is omitted in the imitation between discant and tenor. Cadence is V–I in C.

Pleni.—C, transcribed without diminution throughout this Sanctus.

The *CF* motive, a broken major triad ascending, is the subject of opening imitation in all parts. The *CF* appears sporadically thereafter, until the section close, V–I in C.

Benedictus.—₵.

The same triadal group from the *CF* is the subject of opening imitation, in which the alto participates only briefly. The cadence is IV–I in G.

AGNUS DEI

Source of *CF*: Mass VIII.

Mode: 6 transposed (see footnote 17).

Section

Agnus 2.—⦶ (C in discant is an obvious error), transcribed without diminution. The triadal motive of the *CF* is identical with that of the preceding Sanctus. The parts are simple and the close is V–I in C.

These analytical comments give fair indication of Isaac's incredible contrapuntal facility and inventiveness. Unfortunately, they cannot indicate the superb sound of the music, which has already been proved, at the University of Michigan and elsewhere, in the performance of the *Missa Solemne* and the *Missa Magne Deus*.

If the transcriptions presented here and in the preceding volume (*Choralis Constantinus, Book III*) can bring Isaac belated acclaim, and encourage frequent programming of his music, they will have served their most important purpose.

[17] This transposition raises the pitches a fifth rather than the conventional fourth—once more, no doubt, to avoid tritone relationships.

THE MASSES

The following music was engrossed by Mr. Grant Beglarian.

I. Missa Solemne

[1] Accidentals placed above the note have been supplied by the editor.
[2] The Formschneider edition, hereafter abbreviated F., has F–E for these two bass notes.

Ky- ri - e e- le- i- son
e- le- i- son
le- i- son
e e- le- i- son

— Christe I

Chri - ste
Chri- ste e-
Chri- ste e- le- i-
Chri- ste Chri-

Chri- ste
le - i- son Chri- ste
son e- le- i - son Chri-
ste Chri - ste

e- le- i- son
e- le- i- son e- le- i- son
ste e- le- i- son e- le- i- son
e- le- i- son

— Christe 3

D.
A.
B.
Chri-ste Chri - ste e- le- i-
Chri- ste Chri-
Chri-ste Chri- ste Chri-
son Chri- ste e- le-
ste Chri- ste Chri- ste Chri-
ste Chri- ste Chri- ste Chri -

D.
i- son e- le- i- son
A.
ste e- le- i- son
B.
ste e- le- i- son e- le- i- son

— Kyrie 2b

Ky- ri - e
Ky- ri- e Ky- ri- e e-
Ky- ri - e
Ky- ri - e
Ky- ri- e
le- i - son e- le- i-
Ky- ri- e e- le- i-
Ky- ri- e e- le- i-

e- le- i- son
son Ky- ri- e e- le- i- son
son e- le- i- son
son e- le- i- son

— *Gloria*

Lau- da- mus te
Lau- da- mus te
Lau- da- mus te
Lau- da- mus te

A- do- ra-
A- do- ra-
A- do- ra-
A- do- ra- mus te A- do- ra- mus

mus te
mus te
mus te
te te
Gra- ti- as a- gi- mus ti-
Gra- ti- as a- gi- mus ti-
Gra - ti - as
Gra - ti - as a - gi -
bi ti- bi prop-
bi ti - bi prop-ter ma-
a - gi - mus ti - bi
mus ti- bi prop- ter

ter ma- gnam glo- ri- am tu- am
gnam glo- ri- am tu- am
prop- ter ma- gnam glo- ri- am tu- am
ma- gnam glo- ri- am tu- am
Do- mi- ne Fi-
Do- mi- ne Fi- li u- ni-
Do- mi- ne Fi-
Do- mi- ne Fi-
li u-ni- ge- ni-te Je-su
ge- ni- te u-ni- ge- ni- te Je-su
li u-ni- ge-ni- te Je- su Je-su Je-
li u-ni- ge-ni-te Je- su Je-su Je- su

Chri-
Chri - ste
su Chri-
Chri-ste Chri- ste
ste Al- tis- si- me
Chri- ste Al- tis- si- me
ste Al - tis- si- me
Chri- ste Al- tis- si-me
Qui tol - lis pec-
Qui tol- lis pec-
Qui tol- lis

ca- ta mun- di mun-
ca - ta mun- di mun -
pec - ca- ta mun -
di sus - ci- pe
di sus- ci- pe
di sus- ci - pe
sus - ci- pe
de - pre - ca- ti - o -
de - pre - ca - ti - o -
de - pre- ca - ti- o -
de- pre- ca -

nem no- stram
nem no- stram
nem no- stram
ti- o- nem no- stram
Quo- ni- am
Quo- ni- am tu so-
Quo- ni-
Quo- ni- am tu
tu so- lus san-
lus so- lus
am tu
so- lus

ctus
san- ctus san- ctus san- ctus
so- lus san- ctus
san- ctus
Tu so- lus Al-
Tu so- lus Do-
Tu so-
Tu so- lus Al-
tis- si- mus
mi- nus Tu so-
lus
tis- si- mus Al- tis-

[1]F. has E here.

Al- tis - si - mus Al-
lus Al- tis- si- mus
Al-tis-si- mus Al- tis- si-
si - mus Al- tis - si -
tis - si - mus
Al - tis- si- mus
mus
mus Al- tis- si- mus
Je- su Chri-
Je- su Chri - ste
Je- su Chri- ste
Je - su Chri-

ste Je-su Chri-
Je- su Chri- ste
Je- su Chri-
ste Je- su Chri-
ste
Je- su Chri- ste
ste
ste Chri- ste

— *Credo*

Vi-si-bi-li- um
Vi- si- bi- li- um om-
Vi- si-bi-li- um om-
Vi- si- bi- li- um om- ni- um

om- ni- um et in- vi- si-
ni - um et in- vi- si- bi-
ni - um et in- vi- si - bi -
et in - vi - si -
bi- li- um Et in
li- um Et in u - num Do - mi -
li - um Et in u - num Do- mi - num Je -
bi - li - um Et in u- num
u- num Do- mi- num Je-sum Chri- stum
num Je- sum Chri - stum Chri- stum
sum Chri- stum
Do – mi - num Je - sum Chri- stum

[1]F. has a semibreve here.

Per quem om- ni- a fa- cta sunt Qui prop- ter nos
Per quem om- ni- a fa- cta sunt Qui
Per quem om- ni- a fa- cta sunt Qui prop-
Per quem om- ni- a fa- cta sunt Qui prop-
ho- mi- nes
prop- ter nos ho- mi- nes
ter nos ho- mi- nes
ter nos ho- mi- nes
o=o.
et prop- ter no- stram sa- lu- tem
et prop- ter no- stram sa- lu- tem
et prop- ter no- stram sa- lu- tem
et prop- ter no- stram sa- lu- tem

des- cen- dit de cae- lis
des- cen- dit de cae- lis
des- cen- dit de cae- lis
des- cen- dit de cae- lis
Ex Ma- ri- a Vir-
Ex Ma- ri-
Ex Ma- ri- a
Ex Ma- ri-
gi- ne
a Vir- gi- ne
Vir- gi- ne
a Vir- gi- ne

Et ho-
Et ho-
Et ho-
Et
mo fa-
mo fa-
mo fa-
ho- mo fa-
ctus est
ctus est
ctus est
ctus est

— *Sanctus 2*

[1]F. has a semibreve here.

Be- ne - di - ctus be-ne
Be - ne- di- ctus Be - ne- di - ctus
Be - ne- di - ctus
Be- ne- di - ctus
di - ctus qui
Be- ne- di - ctus Be-ne- di-
Be- ne- di - ctus
o = o·
ve- nit qui ve-
ctus qui ve - nit
qui
qui ve - nit

o· = o
nit in no- mi-
in no-
ve- nit in no- mi- ne Do-
in no- mi- ne
ne Do- mi- ní Do- mi-
mi- ne
mi- ni in no-
Do- mi- ni
ni Do- mi- ni Do- mi- ni
Do- mi- ni
mi- ne Do- mi- ni
Do- mi- ni

— *Agnus Dei 2*

[1]F. has a minima here.

ta mun- di
mun- di
ca- ta mun-
di mi- se- re-
mi- se- re-
mi- se- re- re
di mi- se- re-
re no- bis no-
re no- bis
no- bis
re no- bis
bis

II. Missa Pascale

[1]F. has a semiminima here.

i- son
e- le- i- son e- le- i- son Ky- ri-
le- i- son
ri- e e-
Ky- ri- e e- le- i- son
e e- le- i- son
e- le- i- son
le- i- son e- le- i- son

— *Christe I*

Chri-
Chri- ste e-
Chri-
Chri- ste

ste e-
le- i- son
ste e- le- i- son Chri-
e- le- i- son
le- i- son e- le- i- son
Chri- ste e- le- i- son
ste e- le- i- son
Chri- ste e- le- i- son Chri- ste e- le- i- son

— *Christe 3*

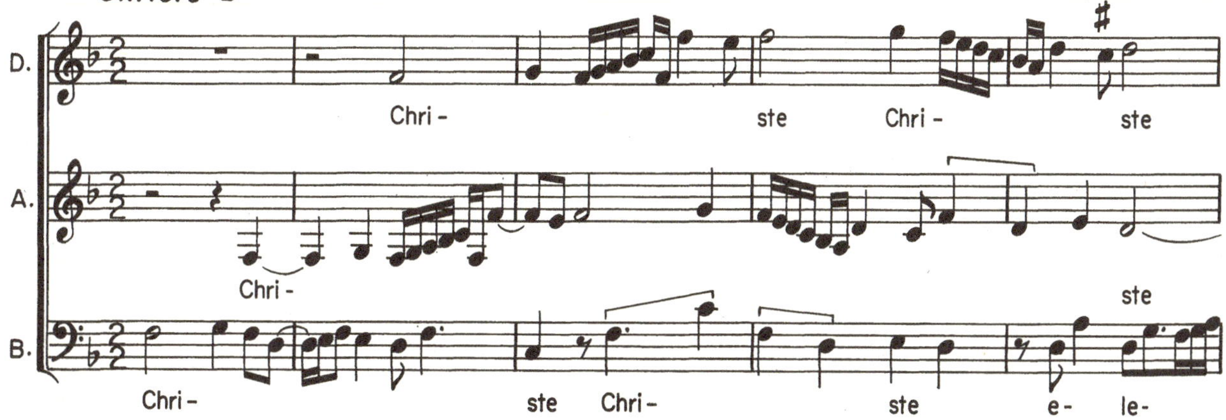
D.
A.
B.
Chri- ste Chri- ste
Chri- ste
Chri- ste Chri- ste e- le-

D.
e- le- i- son e- le-
A.
Chri- ste e- le-
B.
i- son e- le- i- son
i- son e- le- i- son
i- son e- le- i- son e- le- i- son
Chri- ste e- le- i- son

— *Kyrie 2[b]*

Ky- ri- e
Ky- ri- e
Ky- ri- e e
Ky- ri- e Ky- ri-

e- le- i- son
e- le-
le-
e e- le- i-
Ky- ri-e e- le- i-son
i- son Ky- ri- e
i- son e- le- i- son
son Ky- ri- e e- le- i- son

— *Gloria*

Lau- da- mus te
Lau- da- mus te
Lau- da- mus te Lau- da- mus te
Lau- da- mus te

A- do- ra- mus te
A- do- ra- mus te
A- do- ra- mus te
A- do- ra- mus te
Gra- ti- as a-
Gra- ti- as a-
Gra- ti- as a- gi- mus
gi- mus
gi- mus ti-
Gra- ti- as a-
ti- bi ti-

[1]F. lacks one semibreve rest here.

Do- mi- ne Fi-
Do- mi- ne Fi-
li u- ni- ge- ni-
li u- ni- ge- ni-
Je- su Chri- ste
Je- su Chri- ste
te Je- su Chri- ste
te Je- su Chri- ste

Qui tol- lis
Qui tol- lis pec- ca-
Qui tol-
pec- ca- ta
ta mun-
lis pec- ca- ta mun-
mun- di sus- ci- pe
di sus- ci- pe
di sus- ci- pe
sus- ci- pe

de- pre- ca- ti- o- nem no- stram
de- pre- ca- ti- o- nem no- stram
de- pre- ca- ti- o- nem no- stram
de- pre- ca- ti- o- nem no- stram
Quo- ni- am tu so-
Quo- ni- am tu
Quo- ni- am tu so- lus
Quo- ni- am
lus san- ctus san-
so- lus san-
san- ctus san-
tu so- lus san- ctus

ctus san–
ctus san- ctus
ctus san - ctus
san - ctus
ctus san - ctus
san - ctus san - ctus
san - ctus
san - ctus san - ctus
Tu so- lus
Tu so- lus Al- tis- si-

Tu so- lus Al- tis- si- mus
Al- tis- si- mus
Tu so- lus Al- tis- si- mus
mus Al- tis- si- mus
Je - su Je- su Chri -
Je-
Je - su Chri -
Je- su
ste Chri- ste
su Chri- ste Chri - ste
ste Chri - ste
Chri - ste

Et in u- num
Et in u- num Do- mi- num Je- sum Chri-
Et in u- num Do- mi- num Je- sum Chri- stum
Et in u-
Do- mi- num Je- sum Chri- stum
stum Fi- li- um De-
Fi- li- um De- i
num Do mi- num Fi-
Fi- li- um De- i u- ni-
i u- ni- ge-
u- ni- ge-
li- um De- i u- ni-

ge- ni - tum Et ex Pa- tre na- tum an-
ni - tum Et ex Pa- tre na- tum an-
ni - tum Et ex Pa- tre na-
ge - ni- tum Et ex Pa-tre na- tum
te om- ni- a sae- cu- la
te om- ni- a sae- cu- la
tum an- te om- ni- a sae- cu- la
an- te om- ni- a sae -cu- la
Qui prop- ter
Qui prop- ter nos ho- mi- nes
et prop-
et prop-

nos ho- mi-
et prop- ter no- stram
ter no- stram sa- lu-
ter no- stram sa- lu-
nes des- cen- dit de cae- lis
sa - lu - tem des - cen- dit de cae - lis
tem des- cen- dit de cae- lis
tem des- cen- dit de cae - lis
Ex Ma- ri - a Vir - gi-
Ex Ma- ri - a Vir - gi-
Ex Ma- ri - a Vir- gi-
Ex Ma - ri - a Vir- gi-

ne Et ho- mo fa- ctus est
ne Et ho- mo fa- ctus est
ne Et ho- mo fa- ctus est
ne Et ho- mo fa- ctus est
Et re- sur- re- xit
Et re- sur- re- xit ter- ti- a di-
Et re- sur- re- xit ter- ti- a
Et re- sur- re- xit
ter- ti- a di- e se- cun- dum Scrip- tu-
e se- cun- dum Scrip- tu-
di- e se- cun- dum Scrip- tu-
se- cun- dum Scrip- tu- ras

ras Et as-
ras Et as- cen - dit in cae-
ras Et as - cen- dit
Et as- cen- dit in cae -
cen – dit in cae- lum
lum se- det ad dex – te- ram Pa- tris
in cae- lum
lum se- det ad dex- te- ram Pa- tris
Cu- jus
Cu - jus re - gni non
Cu -
Cu- jus re- gni

re- gni non e- rit fi- nis Et in Spi-
e- rit fi- nis Et in Spi- ri-
jus re- gni non e- rit fi- nis fi- nis
non e- rit fi- nis
ri- tum San- ctum Do- mi-
tum San- ctum Do- mi- num
Et in Spi- ri- tum San- ctum
Et in Spi- ri- tum San- ctum Do- mi-
num et
et vi- vi- fi- can- tem
Do- mi- num et
num et vi- vi- fi- can- tem

vi- vi- fi- can - tem
vi- vi- fi- can- tem
Quae pro- ce- dit
Con- fi- te- or
Con- fi- te- or u-
Con - fi- te - or u-
Con- fi- te- or u- num
u- num bap- tis- ma in re- mis- si-
num bap- tis- ma in re-
num bap- tis- ma in re- mis- si- o- nem
bap- tis- ma in re- mis- si - o- nem

o- nem pec- ca- to- rum Et ex- spe - cto re- sur-
mis - si- o- nem pec- ca-to- rum Et ex- spe -
pec- ca-to- rum Et ex -
pec - ca - to- rum Et ex - spe - cto
re - cti-o- nem mor-tu-o - rum
cto re - sur- re - cti- o-
spe - cto re - sur- re - cti - o- nem mor-
re - sur- re - cti - o - nem mor- tu - o-
Et vi- tam ven-
nem mor- tu- o-
tu - o - rum
rum Et vi -

tu- ri sae-
rum Et vi- tam ven- tu-
Et vi- tam ven- tu- ri
tam ven - tu- ri
cu - li
ri sae - cu- li
sae- cu - li
ven - tu - ri sae - cu -
A- men A- men
A- men
A- men
li A- men

— *Sanctus 2*

San-
San-
ctus
San-
San -
ctus
San -
ctus
San -
ctus
San -
ctus
San -
ctus
San -
ctus
D.
A.
B.
Ple -
ni
Ple-
ni
Ple-
Ple-
ni

D.
A.
B.
sunt sunt
ni Ple-
Ple- ni Ple- ni sunt cae-
cae-
ni sunt cae- li et
li et ter- ra
li
ter-
et ter-
et ter- ra
ra glo- ri- a tu-
ra ter- ra ter- ra glo- ri-

[1]F. has two semiminimas here.

ctus
qui ve- nit
nit qui ve- nit ve- nit
ve- nit ve- nit qui ve-
qui ve- nit
qui ve- nit in
ve- nit qui ve- nit
nit ve- nit ve- nit in no- mi-
in no-
no- mi- ne in no- mi- ne
in no- mi- ne no-
ne no-

mi - ne Do - mi - ni
in no - mi - ne Do - mi - ni
mi - ne Do - mi - ni
mi - ne Do - mi - ni

— Agnus Dei 2

A - gnus De - i qui
A - gnus De - i qui
A - gnus De - i qui tol -
A - gnus De - i qui
tol - lis qui tol - lis pec -
tol - lis pec - ca -
lis pec -
tol - lis

ca- ta mun- di mi- se-
ta mun- di mun- di mi-
ca- ta mun- di
pec- ca- ta mun- di pec- ca-
re re mi- se- re-
se- re- re mi- se-re- re
mi- se- re- re no- bis
ta mun- di mi - se- re-
re no- bis no- bis
no- bis no- bis no- bis
re no- bis no- bis no - bis

III. Missa Magne Deus

— *Christe I*

Chri - ste Chri - ste Chri - ste Chri-
Chri - ste Chri - ste Chri- ste e- le - i- son Chri - ste e - lei - son
Chri - ste Chri - ste Chri - ste e - le - i - son e - le - i - son
Chri - ste e - le - i - son e - le - i - son

— *Christe 3*

A.
T.
B.
Chri -
Chri -
ste
Chri -
ste e- le- i- son e-
Chri- ste e- le-
ste e- le- i- son
le- i- son e- le- i- son
i- son e- le- i- son
e- le- i- son

— *Kyrie 2b*

Ky- ri- e e-
Ky- ri- e e- le-
Ky- ri- e
Ky- ri- e
le- i- son Ky- ri- e
i- son
e- le- i- son Ky-
e- le- i- son Ky-
e- le- i- son
Ky- ri- e e- le- i- son
ri- e e- le- i- son
ri- e e- le- i- son e- le- i- son

— *Gloria*

Lau - da-
Lau- da- mus
Lau- da-
Lau-
mus te
te te
mus te
da - mus te
A- do - ra-
A- do- ra - mus te
A- do- ra -
A- do- ra- mus te A-

mus te
te te
mus te
do- ra- mus te
Gra- ti- as a- gi-
Gra- ti- as a- gi- mus
Gra- ti- as a- gi-
Gra - ti - as
mus ti- bi ti- bi prop- ter
ti- bi ti -
mus ti- bi ti- bi ti-
a - gi- mus

ma- gnam ma- gnam ma- gnam glo-
bi ti- bi prop - ter ma-
bi prop- ter ma - gnam ma-
ti- bi prop - ter ma-
ri- am tu- am
gnam glo- ri- am tu- am
gnam glo- ri- am tu- am
gnam glo- ri- am tu- am
Do- mi- ne Fi- li
Do- mi- ne Fi- li u- ni-
Do- mi - ne Fi- li u- ni-
Do - mi - ne Fi - li

u- ni- ge- ni- te Je-su Chri-
ge- ni- te Je- su Chri-
ge-ni-te Je- su Chri- ste
u- ni- ge- ni- te Je- su
ste et San- cte Spi- ri- tus
ste et San- cte
Je- su Chri- ste
Chri- ste et San-
et San- cte Spi- ri- tus et San- cte Spi-ri- tus
Spi-ri- tus Spi- ri- tus
et San- cte Spi- ri- tus
cte Spi- ri- tus Spi- ri- tus

Qui tol- lis pec-ca- ta
Qui tol- lis pec- ca- ta
Qui tol - lis pec- ca- ta mun-
Qui tol - lis pec- ca - ta mun -
mun- di sus-ci -
mun - di sus- ci- pe sus- ci- pe
di sus - ci - pe de-
di mun- di sus-ci -
pe de- pre - ca- ti- o - nem no- stram
de- pre - ca- ti- o- nem no - stram
pre - ca- ti- o- nem no- stram
pe de - pre-ca - ti - o- nem no- stram

Quo- ni - am tu so- lus san- ctus
Quo- ni- am tu so-lus san- ctus
Quo- ni- am tu so-lus san- ctus
Quo- ni- am tu so- lus san- ctus
Tu so- lus Al-tis- si-
Tu so- lus so – lus
Tu so- lus Al- tis- si-
Tu
mus Al-tis- si- mus Je- su Je- su
Al- tis- si- mus Je - su Chri-
mus Je- su
so- lus Do - mi- nus Je - su

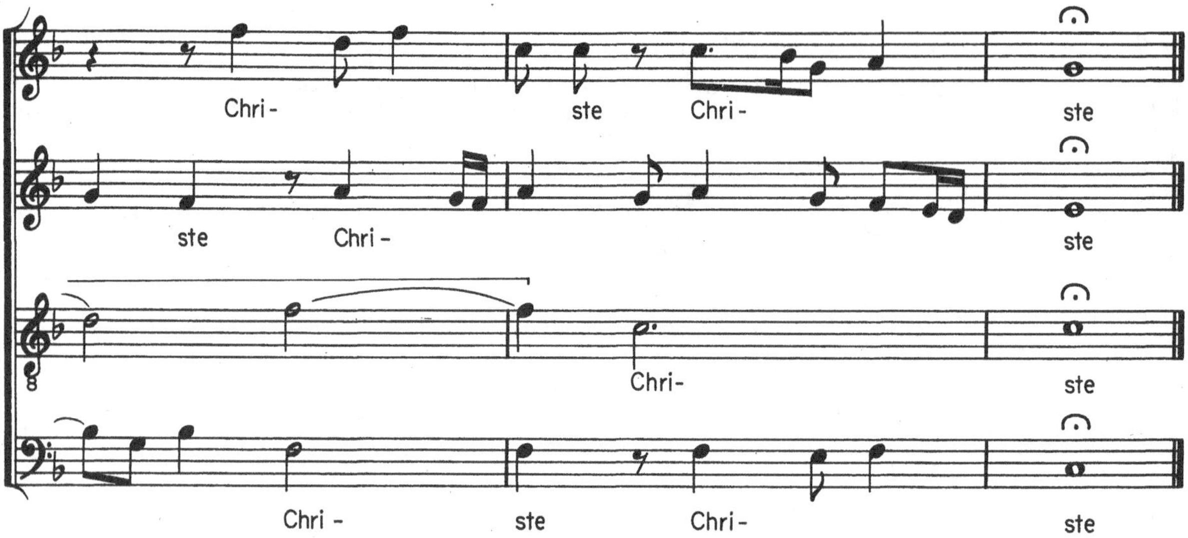
Chri- ste Chri- ste
ste Chri- ste
Chri- ste
Chri- ste Chri- ste

— *Credo*

Et in u- num
Et in u- num
Et in u- num Do- mi- num Je-
Et in u- num Do- mi- num Je-
Do- mi- num Je-
Do- mi- num Je- sum Chri- stum
sum Chri- stum
sum Chri- stum

sum Chri- stum Et ex
Fi- li - um De - i u- ni·- ge- ni - tum Et
Fi - li- um De- i u - ni - ge - ni - tum Et ex
Fi- li - um De- i u- ni - ge - ni - tum Et
Pa - tre na- tum
ex Pa- tre na- tum an- te om- ni- a sae- cu- la
Pa- tre na - tum an- te om- ni- a sae- cu- la
ex Pa- tre na - tum an- te om- ni - a sae- cu- la
Ge - ni - tum non
Ge - ni - tum non fa- ctum non
Ge- ni-
Ge - ni- tum non

fa- ctum con- sub- stan -
fa- ctum
tum non fa -
fa - ctum fa -
ti - a - lem Pa-
con- sub- stan- ti - a - lem
ctum con- sub - stan - ti - a - lem Pa -
ctum con- sub-stan- ti - a -
tri per quem om - ni -
Pa- tri per quem
tri
lem Pa - tri per quem om -

a fa-
om- ni - a fa -
per quem om - ni- a
ni - a fa- cta
cta sunt
cta sunt
fa- cta sunt
fa - cta sunt fa - cta sunt
Ex Ma-
Ex Ma -
Ex Ma- ri - a Ma -

[1]F. has D here.

Ex Ma- ri -
ri- a Vir- gi -
ri- a Vir- gi- ne
ri - a Ma - ri - a Vir -
a Vir - gi - ne
ne Vir - gi - ne
Vir - gi- ne
gi- ne
Et ho - mo
Et ho- mo fa-
Et ho -
Et ho - mo fa -

fa- ctus est
ctus est
mo fa- ctus est
ctus est
Et re- sur- re- xit ter- ti - a di-
Et re- sur- re- xit
e
ter- ti – a di- e se- cun-
Et re - sur- re- xit ter- ti- a di - e
se - cun -

se- cun -
dum Scrip- tu -
se- cun- dum Scrip-
dum Scrip -
dum Scrip- tu - ras
ras Et as- cen- dit
tu - ras
tu - ras Et as-
Et as- cen- dit in cae-
in cae- lum se -
Et as- cen- dit in cae-
cen - dit in cae - lum

lum se- det ad dex- ter-
det ad
lum se- det
se- det
am Pa-
dex- ter- am
ad dex- ter-
ad dex-
tris
Pa- tris
am Pa- tris
ter- am Pa- tris

A.
B.
Et in Spi- ri - tum San- ctum
Et in Spi - ri - tum San - ctum
Do - mi - num et
Do - mi- num
vi - vi- fi - can- tem qui
et vi- vi - fi - can -
pro - ce - . dit
tem qui pro - ce - dit
o = o.
Et u- nam san - ctam ca- tho- li -
Et u - nam san - ctam ca -
Et u- nam san - ctam ca- tho - li -
Et u- nam san- ctam ca- tho- li -

cam et a- pos- to- li-
tho- li- cam et a- pos- to-
cam
cam et a- pos- to- li- cam
cam et a- pos- to- li- cam
li- cam
et a- pos- to- li- cam Ec- cle- si- am
Ec- cle- si- am
o· = o
Ec- cle- si- am
Ec- cle- si- am Con-fi- te-
a- pos-to-li-cam Ec-cle-
et a- pos- to- li- cam Ec- cle- si- am

Con- fi- te- or
or u- num bap- tis- ma in
si- am Con- fi-te-or u- num bap-tis-
Con- fi- te- or u- num bap-tis- ma in
u- num bap- tis- ma re- mis- si- o- nem pec- ca- to- rum
re- mis- si- o- nem pec- ca- to- rum
ma in re-mis-si- o- nem pec- ca- to- rum
re- mis- si- o- nem pec- ca- to- rum

— *Sanctus 2*

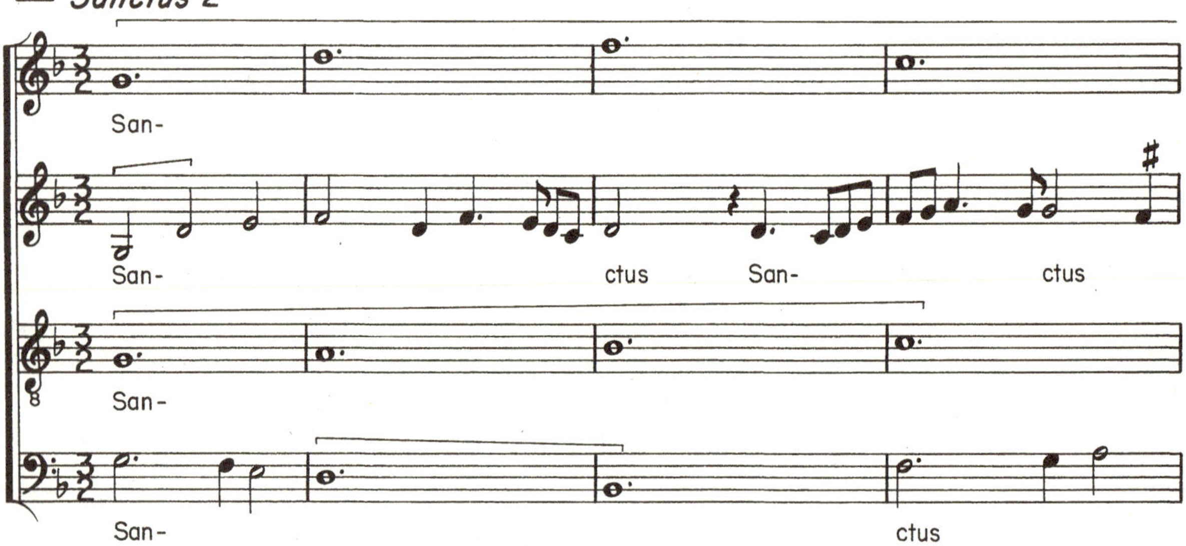
San-
San- ctus San- ctus
San-
San- ctus

ctus
San-
ctus
ctus
San-
ctus
San-
San-
ctus
San-
ctus
San-
ctus
ctus
San-
ctus
San-
ctus

Ple-
Ple- ni sunt· cae-
Ple- ni sunt cae-
Ple- ni
ni sunt cae-
li cae- li
li et ter-
sunt cae- li
li et ter-
et ter-
ra ter- ra et
et ter- ra

ra glo-
ra et ter-
ter- ra glo-
et ter- ra
ri-
ra glo- ri- a
ri- a
glo- ri-
a tu- a
glo-ri- a
tu- a glo-
a tu-

tu- a
tu- a
ri- a tu- a
a tu- a
Be- ne- di-
Be- ne- di-
ctus
qui ve- nit ve-
qui ve- nit

qui
ve -
ctus
qui
ve-
nit
nit
in
nit
ve-
nit
in
no -
no -
in
no -
in
no -
mi-
ne
mi -
ne

mi- ne Do- mi-
mi-
Do- mi- ni
Do- mi- ni
ni Do- mi- ni
ne Do- mi- ni
Do- mi- ni Do- mi- ni
Do- mi- ni

— Agnus Dei 2

A- gnus De-
A- gnus De-
A- gnus
A-

i qui tol- lis qui
i De- i qui tol-
De- i
gnus
tol- lis pec- ca-
lis qui tol-
qui tol- lis pec- ca-
De- i qui tol-
ta mun- di mun-
lis pec- ca- ta pec- ca- ta mun-
ta mun- di mun- di mun-
lis pec-ca- ta pec- ca- ta mun-

di mi- se- re-
di mi- se- re- re mi-
di mi- se-
di mun-
re mi- se-
se- re- re mi- se- re-
re- re mi- se- re- re
di mi- se- re- re
re- re no- bis
re no- bis
no- bis
mi- se- re- re no- bis

IV. Missa de Martyribus

— Christe I

[1]F. lacks the initial two breves of rest, clearly necessary to achieve proper imitative relationship between bass and discant.

— Christe 3

— Kyrie 2b

Ky-
Ky- ri- e e- le- i- son
e- le-
i- son Ky- ri- e
ri- e Ky- ri- e e-
e- le- i- son
1
i- son
e- le- i- son
le- i- son
Ky- ri- e e- le- i- son
Ky- ri- e e- le- i- son
Ky- ri- e e- le- i- son

[1]F. has D here.

Lau- da- mus te
Lau- da- mus te
Lau- da- mus te A- do- ra- mus
Lau- da- mus te A- do- ra-
A- do- ra- mus te
A- do- ra- mus te
te te
mus te
Gra- ti- as a-
Gra- ti- as a-
Gra- ti-
Gra- ti- as a-

gi- mus ti- bi ti-
gi- mus ti- bi
as a- gi- mus ti-
gi- mus ti- bi
bi prop-
prop- ter
bi prop- ter ma_
prop- ter
ter ma- gnam glo-
ma- gnam glo-
gnam glo- ri- am tu-
ma- gnam ma- gnam

ri- am tu- am
ri- am tu- am
am
glo- ri- am tu- am
Do- mi- ne
Do-
Do- mi- ne Fi- li u-
Fi- li u- ni-
mi- ne
ni- ge- ni- te Fi- li u- ni-

ge- ni- te Fi-
Fi- li
ge- ni-
Sa- lus
li u- ni- ge- ni- te Sa- lus
u- ni- ge- ni- te Sa- lus
te u- ni- ge- ni- te Sa- lus
No- stra Je- su Chri- ste
No- stra Je- su Chri- ste
No- stra Je- su Chri- ste
No- stra Je- su Chri- ste

[1]F. has a minima rest here.

sus- ci- pe de-
sus- ci- pe
sus- ci-
sus- ci-
pre- ca- ti- o- nem
de- pre- ca- ti-
pe de- pre- ca- ti- o-
pe de- pre- ca-
de- pre- ca- ti- o- nem no- stram
o- nem no- stram
nem no- stram
ti- o- nem no- stram

D.
Quo - ni - am
A.
Quo - ni-
B.
Quo- ni - am
tu so-
am tu so- lus
tu so- lus san -
lus san - ctus
san- ctus
ctus

Tu so- lus Al-
Tu so- lus Al-
Je- su Chri-
tis- si- mus Je-
tis- si- mus Je-
ste
su Je- su Chri- ste
Je- su Chri- ste
su Chri- ste Chri- ste

— *Credo*

[1]F. has a semibreve here.

cu- la De- um de De-o lu- men de lu- mi-
De- um de De- o lu- men de lu- mi- ne De-
a sae-cu- la De-um de De- o lu- men de lu- mi- ne
De- o lu- men de lu- mi- ne De- um
ne De- um ve- rum de De- o ve- ro
um ve- rum de De- o ve- ro
De- um ve- rum de De- o ve- ro
ve- rum de De- o ve- ro
Qui prop-ter nos ho- mi-nes et prop-ter no-stram sa-
Qui prop- ter nos ho- mi- nes et prop-ter no-stram sa- lu- tem

lu- tem des- cen-
des- cen- dit des- cen-
des-cen- dit de cae- lis
dit de cae- lis
des-cen- dit de cae- lis
dit dc cae- lis
Ex Ma- ri- a Vir- gi- ne Et ho-
Ex Ma- ri- a Vir- gi-
Ex Ma- ri- a Vir- gi- ne

— Sanctus 2

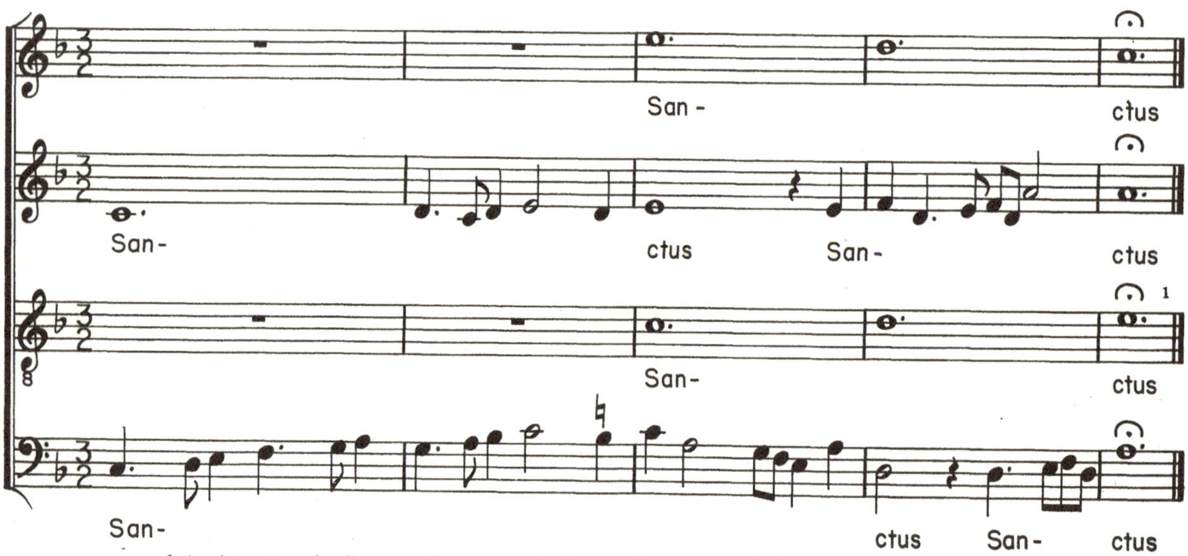

[1] At this point, the discant and tenor part books carry longa rests, which appear to be superfluous.

D.
A.
B.
Ple-
Ple- ni sunt
Ple- ni Ple - ni
ni sunt
cae - li
sunt cae -
cae - li et
et ter-
li et ter-
ter- ra
ra glo-
ra glo- ri-

D.
A.
B.
glo - ri - a tu - a
ri - a tu - a
a tu - a
Be - ne - di -
Be - ne - di - ctus Be -
Be - ne - di - ctus Be -
Be - ne - di - ctus Be - ne -
ctus qui ve - nit
ne - di - ctus Be -
ne - di -
di - ctus qui

ne- di- ctus qui ve-
ctus qui ve- nit ve-
ve- nit
nit ve-
nit
ve- nit ve-
in no- mi- ne
nit in
ve- nit
nit ve- nit in

in no-mi- ne Do- mi-
no-mi- ne in no-mi- ne
in no-mi- ne Do- mi-
no-mi- ne in no- mi-
ni
Do- mi- ni
ni
ne Do- mi- ni

— *Agnus Dei 2*

A- gnus De- i qui tol-lis
A- gnus De- i qui tol-
A- gnus De- i qui tol- lis qui
A- gnus De- i qui tol- lis qui tol- lis

pec- ca- ta mun- di
lis pec- ca.- ta pec- ca- ta mun-
tol- lis pec- ca ta mun- di
pec-ca- ta mun-
mi- se- re- re no-
di mi- se- re- re no- bis
mi- se- re- re no-
dl mi- se- re- rc
bis
no - bis no- bis
bis
no - bis

V. Missa de Confessoribus

— Christe 1

— Christe 3

D.
A.
B.
Chri- ste
Chri- ste
Chri-
e- le-
e- le- i-
ste e- le- i-
i- son
son e- le- i- son
son e- le- i- son
1

[1]F. has E here.

— Kyrie 2b

Ky- ri- e
Ky- ri-
Ky-
e- e e- le- i- son
e e- le- i- son
Ky- ri- e
ri- e e- le-
le- i- son
e- le- i- son
e- le- i- son e- le- i- son
i- son e- le- i- son

Lau- da- mus te
Lau- da- mus te Lau- da- mus te
Lau- da- mus te
Lau- da- mus te
A- do- ra- mus te
A- do- ra- mus te
A- do- ra- mus te
A- do- ra- mus te

[1]F. has D here.

A.
T.
B.
Gra- ti- as a-
Gra- ti- as a- gi-
Gra- ti- as a- gi- mus
gi- mus ti- bi
mus ti-
ti- bi prop- ter
ti- bi prop- ter ma- gnam
bi prop- ter ma- gnam
ma- gnam glo-
glo- ri- am tu- am
glo- ri- am tu- am
ri- am tu- am

Do- mi- ne
Do-
Do- mi- ne Fi-
Do- mi- ne Fi- li
Fi- li u- ni- ge- ni-
mi- ne Fi- li u- ni- ge-
li u- ni- ge- ni-
u- ni- ge- ni-
te Je- su Chri-
ni- te Je- su Chri-
te Je- su Chri-
te Je-- su Chri-

ste Chri - ste Al -
ste Al - tis -
ste Al - tis - si - me Al -
ste Al - tis -
tis - si - me Al - tis - si - me
si - me
tis - si - me
si - me Al - tis - si - me
Qui tol - lis pec - ca - ta
Qui tol - lis pec - ca - ta pec - ca -
Qui tol - lis pec - ca - ta mun - di mun -

[1]F. lacks this note C.
[2]F. has a semibreve here.

D.
A.
B.
tu so- lus
san- ctus san-
tu so- lus san- ctus san-
san- ctus
ctus san- ctus
ctus san- ctus
Tu so-
Tu so- lus Tu so- lus
Tu so- lus
Tu so- lus

lus Al- tis-
Al- tis- si- mus Al- tis- si-
Al- tis-
Al-
si- mus
mus Je- su
si- mus
tis- si- mus
Je- su Chri- ste
Chri- ste
Je- su Chri- ste
Je- su Chri- ste

— *Sanctus 2*

San- ctus
San- ctus
San- ctus
San- ctus
Ple- ni sunt
Ple- ni sunt
Ple- ni
Ple- ni
cae- li cae-
cae-
sunt cae- li
sunt

li et
li cae - li cae -
et
cae - li et ter-
ter- ra
li et ter -
ter - ra
ra glo -
glo - ri - a tu- a
ra glo - ri - a tu - a
glo - ri - a tu - a
ri - a tu - a

Be - ne - di - ctus qui
Be - ne - di -
Be - ne - di
Be - ne - di -
ve - nit in
ctus qui ve -
ctus qui ve - nit
ctus qui ve -
no - mi - ne
nit in no -
in no -
nit in no -

Do-
mi- ne Do- mi-
mi- ne Do- mi-
mi- ne Do-
mi- ni Do- mi- ni
ni
ni
mi- ni

— Agnus Dei 2

A- gnus De- i qui tol-
A- gnus De- i
A- gnus De- i
A- gnus De- i qui tol-

lis tol- lis pec-
qui tol- lis pec- ca- ta pec-
qui tol- lis pec- ca-
lis pec- ca - ta mun-
ca- ta mun- di mi-
ca-ta mun- di mi- se- re-
ta mun-di mi- se- re- re
di mi- se - re -
se- re- re no- bis
re no- bis no-bis no- bis no- bis
no - bis
re no - bis

APPENDIX

PLAIN-SONG SOURCES OF THE *CANTUS FIRMI*

I. Gregorian *Cantus Firmi* for *Missa Solemne*

Kyrie

[GR Mass IV.—*In Festis Duplicibus* 1 (*Cunctipotens Genitor Deus*)]

Gloria

[GR Mass IV.—*In Festis Duplicibus* 1]

Agnus Dei

[*GR* Mass II.—*In Festis Solemnibus* 1]

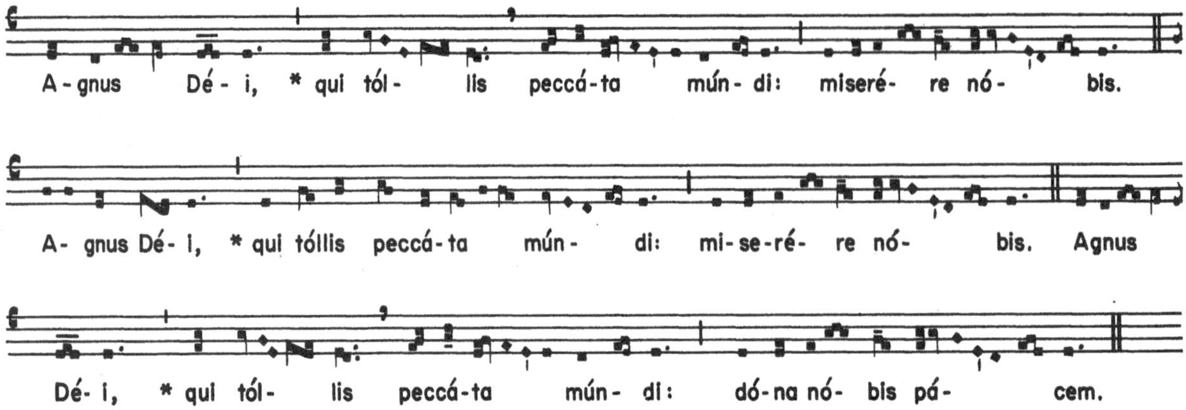

II. Gregorian *Cantus Firmi* for *Missa Pascale*

Kyrie

[GR Mass I.—*Tempore paschali* (*Lux et Origo*)]

Gloria

[GR Mass I.—*Tempore Paschali*]

Sanctus

[GR Mass XVII.—*In Dominicis Adventus et Quadragesimae*]

Agnus Dei

[GR Mass XVII.—*In Dominicis Adventus et Quadragesimae*]

Kyrie

[GR Mass V.—*In Festis Duplicibus* 2 (*Kyrie Magnae Deus Potentiae*)]

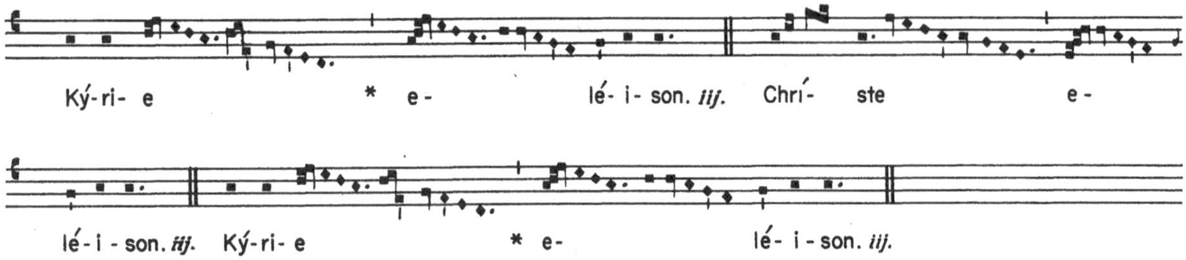

Gloria

[GR *Cantus ad Libitum*.—*Gloria* I]

Sanctus

[GR Mass II.—*In Festis Solemnibus* 1]

Agnus Dei

[GR Mass XV.—*In Festis Simplicibus*]

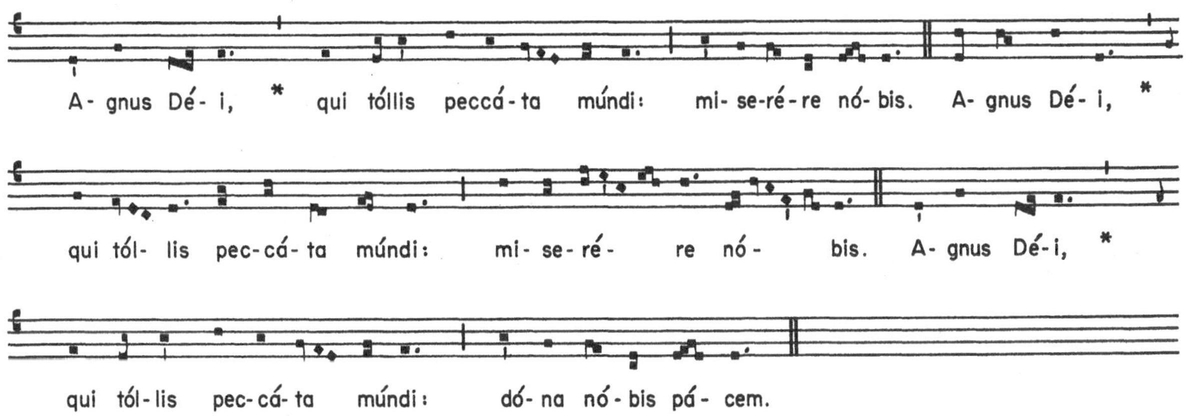

IV. Gregorian *Cantus Firmi* for *Missa de Martyribus*

Kyrie

[GR Mass XI.—*In Dominicis Infra Annum* (*Orbis factor*)]

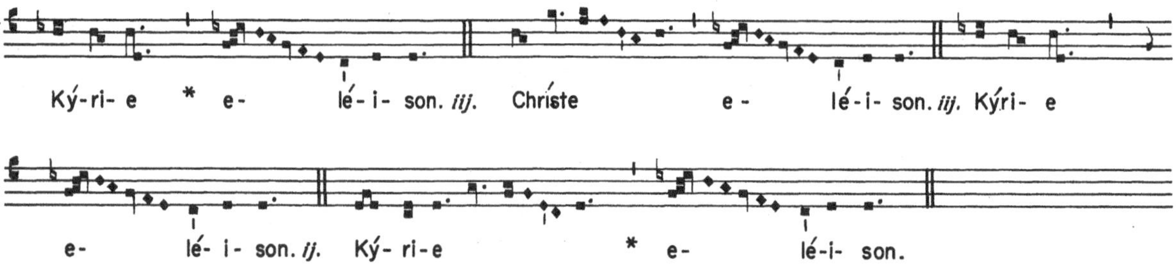

Gloria

[GR Mass II.—*In Festis Solemnibus* 1]

Sanctus

[GR Mass IX.—*In Festis B. Mariae Virginis* 1]

Agnus Dei

[GR Mass IV.—*In Festis Duplicibus* 1]

V. Gregorian *Cantus Firmi* for *Missa de Confessoribus*

Kyrie

[GR Mass XII.—*In Festis Semiduplicibus* 1 (*Pater Cuncta*)]

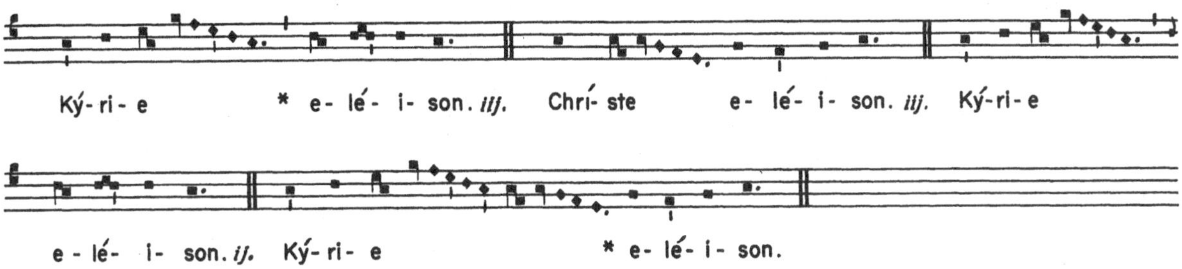

Sanctus

[GR Mass VIII.—*In Festis Duplicibus* 5]

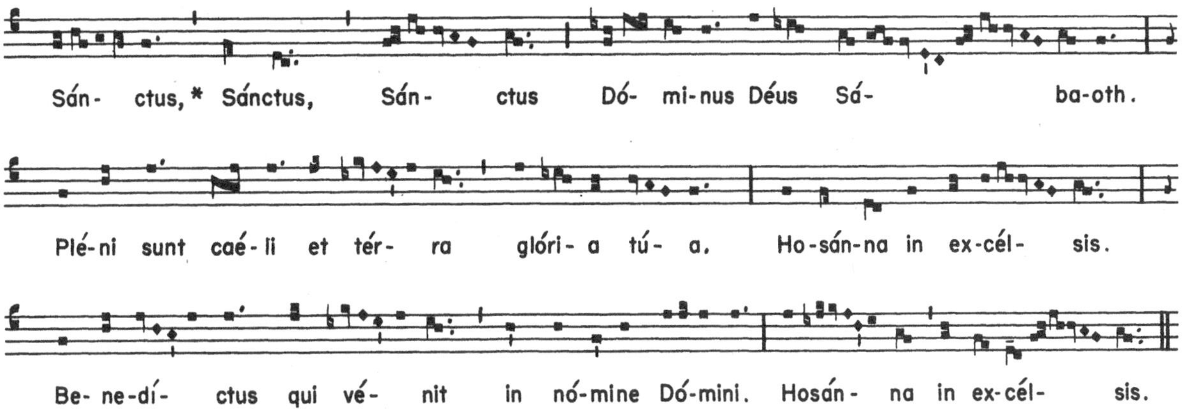

Agnus Dei

[GR Mass VIII.—*In Festis Duplicibus* 5]